Total
Anecdotal

PRAUSPRESS

Total
Anecdotal

A unique and fun guide to help you become a better speaker and writer

Charlie Mechem

Published by Praus Press
Printed in the United States of America
First edition

Library of Congress Cataloging-in-Publication Data

Mechem, Charles Jr. 1930–
  *Total Anecdotal: A Fun Guide to Help You Become
a Better Speaker and Writer*
/ by Charlie Mechem.
p. cm.
  ISBN-13: 978-1-947934-01-6

Cover and interior designed by Stephen Sullivan

Speaking at the White House in the presence of one of the great anecdote users of all time, Ronald Reagan.

Table of

Contents

Acknowledgements

So many people have helped with this book (many of whom are unaware of their help) but I must acknowledge several people who have given me a lot of thoughts and ideas which I truly believe have improved the book significantly.

Pete Strange, the retired Chairman and CEO of Messer Inc., Bob Wehling, the retired Global Marketing and Government Relations Officer of Procter and Gamble have read and critiqued the book and both contributed several anecdotes and other helpful suggestions.

In addition, Jay Stockwell, a very good friend of our family, allowed me to do a "dry run" of a rough manuscript of this book in a speech to his sales force at Neilsen. The group seemed to enjoy the book and that gave me "courage" to go forward.

My deepest thanks to Richard Smucker who wrote a most gracious forward to this book. I served on the Smucker Company Board of Directors for over 25 years and there is no company on the planet for which I have greater respect. Their basic values, their commitment to quality and their unflinching integrity in everything they do should be a model for any company. Richard and his brother Tim took the reins from their legendary father Paul and continued to build this great company. Happily, we stay in touch and I'm honored to call them, and Tim's son, Mark, the current CEO of the Company, my friends.

Next, I truly appreciate the contributions of my publisher Richard Hunt to this book. Richard is a true professional. He is intelligent and thoughtful but, most of all a really nice guy! In this same spirit, my thanks go to Steve Sullivan of Steveco International for his hard and expert work in the formatting of the book. He, too, is a true professional.

And last, but certainly not least, my everlasting thanks to my superb executive assistant, Gretlyn Thomas. She has been tireless and expert in making this book a reality, just as she was with my earlier book, *Who's That With Charlie?* It is no overstatement to say that this book would simply not have happened without Gret!

–CSM

Foreword

We are living in an age of immediate messaging — sound bites, texts, emails, tweets and other social media are changing the way we interact and relate to each other. The spare, quick and brief nature of these exchanges cannot help but influence our overall written and spoken communications. *Total Anecdotal* offers an entertaining and fun perspective on ways to bridge the old and new methods of communicating.

Charlie Mechem, a long-time friend and colleague, has written a unique guide that explains how it is possible to communicate comfortably and effectively adding anecdotes to your communications repertoire. His approach is quite simple yet ingenious, and provides lessons that readers should find easy to adopt and put into practice.

Charlie has vast experience and success with the approach he offers. He has enjoyed an enviable and distinguished career as a partner in the law firm of Taft Stettinius & Hollister, the Chairman and

CEO of Taft Broadcasting Company, Commissioner of the Ladies Professional Golf Association, and was a valuable Board Member at The J. M. Smucker Company for more than a quarter century. It was during his time with our company that I watched him practice his extraordinary communications skills. He was one of the most masterful communicators it has been my privilege to know and work with.

In *Total Anecdotal*, Charlie passes along the secrets of his unique approach to communicating. He clearly demonstrates how anecdotes and stories can help to effectively relay messages with humor and emotion to better connect on a more personal level. *Total Anecdotal* is a valuable addition to expanding one's communications arsenal, and I think you will enjoy Charlie's wit and stories along the way.

Richard Smucker
Executive Chairman
The J. M. Smucker Company

A Word from
the Author

A brief word about my background might be helpful to the reader. I was born in 1930 and raised in the small town of Nelsonville, Ohio. By the way, I was by no means the most important thing that happened in 1930. You should know that was the year Twinkies, Wonder Bread and Snickers bars were introduced to the American public. I'm just happy to be in such illustrious company.

After graduating from Nelsonville High School, Miami University in Oxford, Ohio and the Yale Law School, I was blessed to have several quite different careers. I practiced law for ten years, was CEO of an important broadcasting and entertainment company (Taft Broadcasting Company), served as Commissioner of the Ladies Professional Golf Association, acted as Board Chairman of several sizeable corporations and was personal advisor to a number of professional golfers including Arnold Palmer, Jack Nicklaus, Nancy Lopez, Juli Inkster, Annika Sorenstam and Dottie Pepper. (I hope the reader will not regard this as "name-dropping" or "company-dropping." Instead, the purpose is simply to make clear the very different character of my different activities.)

Because of the significant differences in each of these "careers," I had the opportunity to meet a wide variety of people and make speeches to groups of all sizes and shapes. I developed my own speaking style, one which relies heavily on anecdotes to illustrate and underscore the points I was trying to make. Whenever I could, I tried to make these anecdotes humorous, feeling that this would make them even more memorable. I am convinced that this works.

Some of the greatest speakers in history used anecdotes effectively. Exhibit A is Abraham Lincoln. In his magnificent biography "Lincoln" by David Herbert Donald, the author states, "In the courtroom Lincoln maintained a personal connection, seeming to speak to each juror individually and in a conversational tone. He rarely used technical language, *and he was a master of the homespun anecdote to illustrate his point.*" (Italics mine)

Another example is Ronald Reagan, another president who used anecdotes frequently and they were almost always humorous.

The greatest thing that has happened to me in my life has been my marriage to Marilyn Brown, my Miami University sweetheart. We have three great kids and five wonderful grandchildren. This whole gang continues to inspire me and keep me very humble.

Three closing thoughts. First, you will see that some of the anecdotes involve experiences from my life. If one or more of these stories helps you express or underscore a point you are trying to make, you should not feel it necessary to use my name. The stories themselves make the point and it is the point that is important — not me!

Second, some might say that some of the entries in this book are not, strictly speaking, anecdotes but, rather, are simply jokes. I plead guilty to this transgression, but offer a defense. The dictionary defines an anecdote as "a short account of an entertaining or interesting incident." I think a joke qualifies under that definition. Whether it does or doesn't, I'm including them because I have found that a good joke can illustrate and underscore a point very effectively.

Third, a friend who read the manuscript of this book suggested that it would be appropriate to begin the book with an anecdote. This is a wonderful idea and I think have just the story to fit the bill.

I once had a friend who served as CEO of one of the great old industrial companies — Carborumdum. This was a classic heavy-industry concern that made grinding wheels, abrasives, etc. The businesses that we respectively ran could hardly have been more different, and that undoubtedly had something to do with our friendship. One day, he called me to say that he was coming through Cincinnati and wondered if we could get together. I told him I would love to see him and would take him on a tour of our Kings Island amusement park (where we could also have lunch). We were almost finished with the tour when he said to me, "Let me get this straight. Your company owns radio and televisions stations, owns the Hanna Barbera Cartoon Company, builds and operates amusement parks and is involved in the production of television shows and motion pictures." I replied that indeed this was the essence of our business. He smiled and said, "Sounds like a lot of fun. Do you get paid in your job?" We both had a good laugh, but as I reflected on his comment I realized how fortunate I had been to be involved with an enterprise that was dedicated to educating and entertaining people in all walks of life. Maybe I shouldn't have gotten paid after all. But, it's too late now for a refund — I've already spent the money!

So, now, let's get on with it.

What Is This Book About?

This book was inspired by a conversation that I had a couple of years ago with my son-in-law, Ted Doering. I had just finished writing a book called *"Who's That With Charlie?"* which is a reminiscence of the many wonderful people who I've had the privilege of knowing over my eighty-plus years. Ted remarked that now that I had finished that book, he had a suggestion for my next book.

I wasn't sure that I was ready for a second book, but I was intrigued so I asked him what he had in mind. He explained that he had observed over the years that I frequently used anecdotes in speaking and writing to emphasize points that I was trying to make. I acknowledged that this was my style and that I felt strongly that the people listening to you or reading something you had written were more likely to remember the point you are trying to make if you illustrate it with an anecdote — preferably a humorous one. Hence, this little book.

The organization of the book is quite simple. I catalog a number of issues, categories, points — call them what you will — then offer several anecdotes relevant to the particular subject. So, if you are making a speech or preparing a written presentation, you can look through the list and see if there are anecdotes that will be useful in making your case. Obviously, I have not included everything that you might need, but hopefully, the subjects that I have included and the accompanying anecdotes will be helpful.

A Few Tips on Effective Communication

Before getting into the heart of the book, it's important to say a word about effective communication. Being able to communicate clearly, either spoken or written, has never been more challenging than it is today. So many of the modern techniques — e-mailing, texting, blogging, tweeting, etc. — have led to a very different style of communication than has historically been the case. The overriding goal of these techniques seems to be brevity which, I fear, is often accomplished at the expense of spelling, good grammar, meaning and clarity. Moreover, there is often a confrontational tone, especially in blogs. So, my point is that it's worth spending a little time talking about *how* to get your message across clearly and in a manner that the listener or reader will enjoy. After all, if you don't master the mechanics of effective communication, the content of your message won't much matter!

To me, effective communication consists of two principal elements — *what* you say and *how* you say it. Truly effective communication requires both — one can't stand without the other. This book is about helping you say what you want to say in a manner that your audience will both understand and enjoy.

But, first, let's briefly deal with the other essential element — *how* to convey your message. Now, I don't intend to spend a lot of time on this because there are many fine books and articles on the art of public speaking. I'm simply going to share with you what has worked for me over more than sixty years and in countless speeches and presentations. Much of what I am going to suggest, of course, is primarily applicable to the spoken word, but I think it also has relevance to a written presentation as well.

Let's talk about something very mundane but extremely important, namely, what you take with you to the podium — if anything. Will your presentation be extemporaneous, from a written manuscript or with the help of some notes? The decision on which of these approaches to employ will obviously depend on the occasion and the audience. If you are speaking to a small group in an informal setting, extemporaneous might work. I say "might" because even in this setting speaking "off the cuff" is risky. Why? Two reasons: First, if you get flustered or lose your train of thought, confusion and embarrassment — or worse — will follow. I once saw a very bright and accomplished man lose his train of thought while introducing a major political figure to a large audience. He had no notes and became so flustered and embarrassed that he literally fainted. Second, you may simply forget some important points by not having notes to remind you. So, extemporaneous might work...but you had better be good at it!

The opposite tack is a full manuscript. This is a fail-safe in terms of communicating precisely, but it runs the risk of losing the audience because you are simply reading your speech. Unless you can do it extremely well, it may diminish the real force of what you are trying to say. Sometimes, of course, speaking from a written manuscript is necessary. If you are dealing with an audience or a subject where you might be quoted — or misquoted — then a written manuscript is a necessity. However, for most people this will rarely be the case.

This leads me to my favorite approach — bullet point type notes. Using bullet point type notes on index cards (or whatever) is an appropriate compromise between extemporizing and reading. It makes it very difficult for you to lose your place and forget something, but allows you to keep eye contact with the audience and gives your remarks an informal and friendly quality without the risks noted above. One of the masters of this approach was Arnold Palmer. I had the honor and pleasure of working closely with Arnie for many years, and was often with him when he gave speeches or did press conferences. He always used 5 x 7 cards with bullet points for the essential comments that he wanted to make. If you ever saw Arnie speak, you know that his presentations were smooth and effortless. This was not an accident. He prepared carefully and the 5 x 7 cards allowed him flexibility to communicate the important points, while at the same time, permitting him the easy, informal style for which he was so well known. This was his practice, with the assistance of his longtime associate Doc Giffin, for many years.

Now, let's turn to what I think of as the mechanics of speech making. I took several speech classes in high school and college, and I learned a lot. Amazingly though, the best advice I ever got was from my grandfather. He was a coal miner all his life, as well as the head usher at the little church we attended in Nelsonville, Ohio. During my early teenage years, I attended a church camp virtually every summer. Upon return, I'd be asked to speak to the Sunday morning congregation and share our experiences at camp. My grandfather pointed out that his job as head usher required him to stay in the back of the church and that he could be hard of hearing. So, he said, "Please speak slowly and loudly so that I can hear every word. Be sure to enunciate, and pause briefly between each sentence."

Let me elaborate a bit on a couple of these points. Speaking slowly is not as easy as it might seem and most people speak faster than they realize. It is important to consciously slow yourself down. When you do that you will actually be speaking at a pace that will seem quite normal to the listeners. Equally important is to pause briefly between each sentence. To put it another way, make a conscious effort to "put a period" at the end of every sentence. One of the biggest mistakes that I hear people make is to end a thought with something other than a period — perhaps an "and" or a "but." The problem with this is that you are basically compelling yourself to continue and frequently you have no idea how to do that because there really is nothing more to the thought.

This leads to one of several results — none of them good. One is to stutter or stammer because you really have nothing with which to complete the sentence. Thus, there will be a long string of "uhs" and "ahs." Another is that in a desperate attempt to complete the sentence, you might make some inane remark which makes absolutely no sense. If you mentally put a period at the end of each sentence, this problem will not occur.

Finally, let's talk about how to begin your speech. Why? Because a good introduction does two things: first, it provides a thumbnail sketch of what you intend to talk about and, second, it gives you the chance to interject some humor into your remarks. The reason this is important is that, if you can get the audience to laugh or smile right away, they'll think "This guy seems like he's going to be OK" or "I think I'm going to enjoy listening to this gal."

So, let me suggest to you six ways to introduce your remarks. These have worked well for me over the years and I hope you will find them helpful.

Introductions:
That was a very nice introduction and probably more generous than I deserve. Nevertheless, it is one that my father would have enjoyed hearing and my mother would have believed!

Well, that was a very flattering introduction. Indeed, after that introduction, I can hardly wait to hear what I have to say!

I'm delighted to be with you. We each have a job to do today. My job is to speak, yours is to listen. If you finish your job before I finish mine, please raise your hand.

You look like a really good audience. Someone once said that the best audience that any speaker could have would be one that was intelligent, interested in your subject and just a little drunk. I can't tell whether you possess any of these qualities, but I'm hoping for at least two out of three!

This has been a long evening and I will keep my remarks brief. There's a wonderful story about a man who was the last speaker on a crowded after-dinner agenda. By the time he rose to speak, he unfortunately was inebriated. On his way to the podium, he stumbled and fell on the floor - flat on his back. After a couple of failed attempts to rise, he turned his head to the audience and said, "I believe I will dispense with my prepared remarks and simply take questions from the floor."

Occasionally you will find yourself on a program with some very well-known people. When I have been confronted with such a situation I have used this line which always works. This is a very impressive head table. Indeed, as I look up and down the dais, I am the only one here that I have never heard of before!

Here's a tip that can be very useful as you begin your talk. Keep your eyes and ears open from the moment you enter the room. The odds are good that you will notice something that you can use in your introduction that the audience will also have seen or heard. This will serve to make the audience more comfortable with you because they are in on the joke. Let me give you two examples.

Some years ago, at a black-tie dinner in Cincinnati at which I was to speak, the dessert that was served consisted of pears with a frozen chocolate shell. The problem was that the pears and chocolate had been left in the freezer too long. When they were served, they were still frozen. The result was that when someone attempted to cut them, more often than not they simply slid off the plate, often onto the floor with a very audible sound. It was like hockey pucks flying around. Everyone was embarrassed, but no one said a word. When I got up to speak, I said how pleased I was to be there but then I added, "Before we begin, would everyone whose frozen pear is not already on the floor, please put it there so I can go on with my remarks. Well, the room erupted in laughter and it made the whole relationship with the audience a warmer, closer one from the beginning.

Another wonderful example. The LPGA had a tournament in Lansing, Michigan, sponsored by Oldsmobile. Lansing was always an important automobile center, and everything about the town reflected that. I arrived in Lansing for the tournament one year and learned that there had just been a spirited and somewhat controversial contest to decide on a name for the new Lansing Minor League Baseball franchise that everyone was very excited about. The name ultimately chosen in the contest was a beauty—the Lansing Lugnuts! Lugnuts, for those of you who don't know, are the nuts that hold the tires onto your car. I don't know why they're called lugnuts, but that's what they're called. The logo showed a whirling lugnut with a sort of sadistic little grin. Many people were happy about the name, but some weren't.

As I had just arrived in town that day, nobody thought that I even knew about this matter. I was so amused by the whole thing that at the Pro-Am dinner when I was asked to make some remarks, I said how happy I was to be in Lansing and that I was always treated well. But, I said, at dinner a little earlier, a troublesome thing had occurred and I wasn't sure why. When eating my dessert, I bit down on something hard, and though it didn't break my teeth, it frightened me. I got it out of my mouth and looked at it, it was a lugnut! Then, I said, "Why in the world would there be a lugnut in my dessert?" (Of course, I was making this up.) Well, the whole crowd went crazy because, again, they hadn't expected me to know anything about the controversy. There had been a lot of tension over the choice of the name, and when I made this comment, it seemed to relieve some of that tension. Anyway, I'll never forget it, and I have a hat hanging in my office today with the little Lansing Lugnut logo on it. A wonderful Lansing memory.

Just a few more suggestions on how best to deliver remarks.

Avoid unnecessary words — "so", "like", "you know" and so forth. These words and phrases are increasingly a part of the American vocabulary and while they might work in everyday conversation, they don't work in prepared remarks.

Don't try to impress people with "big" words. They may not understand such words but even if they do, your remarks will appear condescending.

Be sure and adapt your vocabulary to the audience with whom you are speaking. Don't lapse into language or jargon that is unfamiliar to your audience.

Don't force gestures. Let gestures come naturally. If they don't come naturally, don't use them. It is better to have no hand or arm gestures than it is to force them.

Now that we've gone over how best to deliver your remarks, let's have some fun as we turn to the primary subject of this book — a collection of anecdotes that will help you make your point.

The Anecdote Glossary

Adaptability & Flexibility

This story is very special to me as it was Neil Armstrong's favorite joke. Although, I'm not sure he ever finished it, primarily because he would begin to laugh uncontrollably before he got to the end. I have used it a number of times to highlight the importance of flexibility and being quick on one's feet.

Two guys were walking down the street on a very hot and humid day. Each had their dog and were enjoying their stroll...except for one thing. They were both thirsty. One fellow said to the other, "I'm dying for a beer." The other fellow replied, "So am I and — look — we're in luck, there's a bar." They started to enter the bar when one of the guys noticed a sign in the window that read — in bold black letters — no dogs allowed! At first, they were devastated, then one guy said, "I've got an idea. I'll go inside and if the bartender challenges me, I'll simply say this is my seeing-eye dog. If I'm not back here in five minutes, then you will know it's safe for you to come in." The other guy said, "Sounds like a great idea." So, the first guy goes in the bar, and the bartender immediately says, "Hey buddy, you can't come in here with that dog. No dogs allowed." The guy responds, "Oh, I'm so sorry, sir. But I'm blind and this is my seeing-eye dog." Well, the bartender is embarrassed and says, "I'm so sorry. I didn't realize. Let me help you over to the bar, and the beer's on the house." Meanwhile, five minutes have gone by and the guy who stayed outside decides that the coast is clear, so he walks into the bar with his dog. The bartender says, "What's going on here? Can't you read? No dogs allowed!" The fellow says, "I'm very sorry, sir. I didn't know about the no-dog rule because I am blind, and this is my seeing-eye dog." The bartender says, "Wait just a minute, buddy; that's a Chihuahua." Without missing a beat, the guy says, "WHAT? They gave me a Chihuahua?!"

❖   ❖   ❖   ❖   ❖

This is a very effective story to tell when emphasizing the importance of adapting quickly to a surprising development.

It seems that a young man had just started working in a grocery store. On his very first day, a man came in and said, "Son, I'd like to buy a half a head of lettuce." The young boy thought this was very strange, but following the theory that the customer is always right, he took a knife and sliced the head in half, wrapped the half, and gave it to the gentleman. Thinking that the man had left the store, he turned to one of the other clerks and said, "Boy, that nutty guy wanted half a head of lettuce." He then realized to his dismay that the man had not left the store, but was standing right behind him. Quickly he said to the other clerk, "Fortunately, this fine gentleman wanted to buy the other half." The manager had heard this exchange and came up to the young man and said, "That was an amazing display of flexibility and adaptability. You might have a real future in this store. Tell me about yourself." The young man replied, "Well, there really isn't much to tell. I'm only seventeen years old. I just came from Lost Moose up in Canada, but I just had to get out of Lost Moose because there is nothing there but hockey players and hookers." The manager frowned and said, "Just a minute, young man, my wife is from Lost Moose." Without missing a beat, the young man said, "Is that so? What position did she play?"

❖   ❖   ❖   ❖   ❖

I have used the following line when I am pointing out the importance of being adaptable. This line brings some needed balance and underscores that some things never change.

Not everything can or should be adaptable or flexible. Thomas Watson, the founder of IBM once said, "We can and will change everything — except our values."

❖   ❖   ❖   ❖   ❖

"There is nothing more difficult to take in hand, more perilous to conduct, or more uncertain in its success than to take the lead in the introduction of a new order of things." — *Niccolo Machiavelli*

❖   ❖   ❖   ❖   ❖

Groucho Marx is reported to have said, "The secret of life is honesty and fair dealing. If you can fake that, you've got it made."

❖   ❖   ❖   ❖   ❖

This is a totally true story. I have used it many times when trying to make the point that a sense of humor can often soften what would otherwise be an awkward moment.

I was privileged to serve for more than twenty-five years on the Board of the J. M. Smucker Company. Paul Smucker was CEO and driving force throughout the years, an extraordinary man in many ways. One year during the question-and-answer period at the annual meeting, a woman got up, noted that she and Paul had known one another since they were in grade school together, and that she had always loved the company and everything it stood for. But, she said, "There is one little thing. Paul, all of your jams and jellies are put up in such large jars. We older folks, especially those of us living alone, don't need such big containers. Couldn't you put up your jams and jellies in itty-bitty jars?" The audience laughed and applauded. I thought, wow, how is Paul going to handle this one? It was a good question and it was asked by a lovely lady and an old school friend. Paul smiled and said, "Mabel, you're right. We've known one another for many years, and I respect your judgment. It's a very good question that you've asked. Let me try to answer this way. We could, indeed, and maybe should, put up our jams and jellies in itty-bitty jars. But, Mabel, if we did, then we'd have to pay itty-bitty dividends!" The audience roared, Mabel smiled, and the meeting went on.

❖   ❖   ❖   ❖   ❖

One of the great business minds belonged to the late Peter Drucker. He had more words of wisdom on business than any author I have read.

Here is what he had to say regarding change: "We no longer even understand the question whether change is, by itself, good or bad. We start out with the axiom that it is the norm. We do not see change as altering the order — we see change as being order in itself — indeed the only order we can comprehend today is a dynamic, a moving, a changing one."

❖   ❖   ❖   ❖   ❖

It is reported that Napoleon in addressing James Watt regarding his invention of the steam engine said, "What have you done, sir? You wish to improve my ships by lighting a bonfire beneath their decks! What folly!"

Age

I have used this anecdote over and over again with older groups. They love it for obvious reasons. Not that it wouldn't work for a younger audience but it's a home run with older audiences.

An eighty-five-year-old lady was visiting her doctor because she had been feeling tired and listless. After examining her, the doctor called her into his office and said, "Madam, I have unbelievable news — you're pregnant!" She, of course, was horrified and said, "But that's impossible. I'm eighty-five and my husband is ninety-three." The doctor nodded and said, "I understand that you are shocked, but I have run all the tests and it is very clear — you're going to have a baby." The distraught lady called her husband on the phone. When he answered, she practically yelled at him, "Henry, you got me pregnant!" After a brief pause, her husband replied, "Who's this calling?"

❖   ❖   ❖   ❖   ❖

One fellow said to another, "I can do the same things now at age seventy that I did when I was sixteen." The other fellow observed, "Really? You must have had a lousy childhood!"

❖   ❖   ❖   ❖   ❖

The great Danish pianist/comedian Victor Borge once commented, "I'm really embarrassed about this big occasion celebrating my sixty-fifth birthday. I'm embarrassed because I'm really seventy-five."

❖   ❖   ❖   ❖   ❖

This anecdote is very appealing to groups of young people. I think this is because they have never really thought of aging in this manner.

Don't be so smug, young people. One day you too will wake up and not recognize anyone on the cover of *People.*

❖   ❖   ❖   ❖   ❖

Jonathan Swift is supposed to have said, "Every man desires to live long! Yet no man desires to be old."

❖   ❖   ❖   ❖   ❖

Adlai Stevenson once said, "Nothing so dates a person as to decry the younger generations."

❖   ❖   ❖   ❖   ❖

This is not really an anecdote. Rather it is my thoughts on the stages of a typical career. It works particularly well for an older audience, some of whom will have reached stages five or six. But you can use this with a younger audience as well by asking them at what stage they believe they are. The stages are as follows:

Stage One: Overwhelming naiveté mixed with puppy-like eagerness
Stage Two: Mindless panic as reality dawns and a crushing workloads descend
Stage Three: Thrilling discovery that most successful people are lucky rather than smart
Stage Four: Success without recognition or reward
Stage Five: Recognition and reward without success

Stage Six: Undeserved honors from those who forgive and forget

Stage Seven: The gradual, but irreversible, decline into irrelevancy.

Stage Eight: Oblivion

❖   ❖   ❖   ❖   ❖

This is a fun anecdote to use with a group of widely varying ages. After reciting the anecdote, it is fun to ask them which of the groups they believe they fit into.

A group of 40-year-old buddies discuss where they should meet for dinner. Finally, it is agreed upon that they should meet at the Gausthof zum Lowen restaurant because the waitresses there are friendly and pretty.

Ten years later, at 50 years of age, the group meets again and once again they discuss where they should meet. Finally, it is agreed upon that they should meet at the Gausthof zum Lowen because the food there is very good and the beer selection is great.

Ten years later at 60 years of age, the group meets again and once again they discuss where they should meet. Finally, it is agreed upon that they should meet at the Gausthof zum Lowen because they can eat there in peace and quiet.

Ten years later, at 70 years of age, the group meets again and once again they discuss where they should meet. Finally, it is agreed upon that they should meet at the Gausthof zum Lowen because the restaurant, and especially the restroom, is wheelchair-accessible.

Ten years later, at 80 years of age, the group meets again and once again they discuss where they should meet. Finally, it is agreed upon that they should meet at the Gausthof zum Lowen because they have never been there before.

One sure sign of aging is when an increasing number of items that you get back from the dry cleaners say, "The remaining stain or discoloration in this garment have been carefully examined. Further attempts to remove them might cause damage to the color or fabric." I never saw such a note until just a few years ago!

I had a wonderful joke pulled on me when I turned eighty. A friend said, "How old are you?" I replied, "80." He said, "That's absolutely incredible." I naturally assumed that this was a compliment and that he felt that I didn't appear eighty. But he then said, "I thought you were at least 90." A great putdown. This is not only an anecdote about age but also the very human tendency to sometimes getting "puffed up" without reason.

Someone once said that birthdays, like golf, are so much more fun when you don't keep score.

The following is an old joke, but always gets a laugh. It's worth having in your repertoire.

There was an aged man sitting on the curb crying. A stranger asked him what was wrong. The old man said, "Last year, I won millions in the lottery. Six months ago, I finished my dream house. Last week, I married a beautiful, young model who is waiting at home for me." The stranger said, "That's all wonderful, why are you crying?' The old man looked at him and said, "I'm crying because I can't remember where I live."

Arrogance

This is especially effective when speaking to a group of high achievers — young and old — who might need a reminder that they are not omnipotent. It's the story of a ship's captain as told by Frank Koch in "Proceedings" the magazine of the Naval Institute.

One night at sea, the captain saw what looked like the light of another ship heading toward him. He had his signalman signal to the other ship. He said, "Change your course ten degrees south." The reply came back, "Change your course ten degrees north." Well, the captain answered, "I am a captain. Change your course south." To which the reply was, "Well, I'm a seaman, change your course north!" This, of course, infuriated the captain so he signaled back, "DAMN IT! I say change your course south. I'm on a battleship!" To which the reply came back, "I say change your course north. I'm in a lighthouse!"

❖   ❖   ❖   ❖   ❖

Mark Twain quote: "It ain't what you don't know that gets you in trouble. It's what you know for sure that just ain't so."

❖   ❖   ❖   ❖   ❖

Someone once said that the best advice he could give is that you try not to be in a room with more than one person at a time who thinks he is Jesus.

Art of Negotiation

Whatever our job or position, all of us are involved in negotiations of one sort or another. Here are a few stories that may help you, directly or indirectly, or that can form the basis of advice that you give to others.

A good piece of advice — listen to the older, wiser heads — those who have "been there" before. One of the best examples — and certainly the funniest — that I can give on this point involved the CEO of a major company with whom Taft Broadcasting had a joint venture. The chairman, Jake Davis, was an unforgettable character who had been a good friend of my father's and was wonderful to me when we moved to Cincinnati. I remember him for many reasons, but probably more than any other is something he said to me which I have never forgotten and which I have put into practice more than once. I was in his office and we were discussing some sort of business proposal that we were planning to make to another company. I had some ideas but he felt I was being too generous. He outlined a proposal which I thought was outrageously favorable to our side. I said, "We can't offer that kind of a deal — it's too one-sided." He smiled and said, "Charlie, let me tell you something. Never be ashamed to offer a guy a lousy deal." Shocking perhaps — but words of wisdom!

❖　　❖　　❖　　❖　　❖

Another example of how a sense of humor can smooth out what otherwise might be a "sticky" situation came during a negotiation that I was having with Jack Schiff, one of Cincinnati's toughest and smartest business leaders. He had built a superb financial institution and he was extraordinarily shrewd. Jack was in my office one day to discuss some business arrangement that our two companies were developing. I don't remember the nature of the transaction but it is not important to the story. As we exchanged thoughts, I made a proposal which was definitely slanted to my advantage. Perhaps being influenced by Jake Davis' admonition, it was definitely slanted to our advantage. Jack looked at me for a minute, then smiled and said, "Charlie, if I were to accept that proposal, you would be entitled to at least a full chapter in the New Testament!" I don't remember for sure but my guess is that I blushed and quickly changed the subject.

The brilliant financier Meshulam Riklis put it this way: "You can name the price if I can name the terms."

I approach a negotiation as a discussion that leads to making a deal. As a result, I have always felt that respect for the other party and willingness to compromise were essential ingredients. If one does not treat the other party with respect and courtesy it is harder to reach an agreement. Similarly, if one is unwilling to compromise, it is hard to see how an agreement can be successfully reached. It's like the old saying goes — a successful deal will not totally please either party.

I am very opposed to the opposite approach, the approach that sees negotiating as "winning" and humiliating your adversary. Again, negotiating should not be about winning, but rather reaching a satisfactory agreement and maintaining a relationship with the other party that will permit you to remain friendly and respectful in the future. I have never been more convinced about the rightness of my approach as

I have been recently as we have watched the hopelessness and craziness of the negotiations in Washington over the debt ceiling and the so-called fiscal cliff, not to mention immigration and a host of other issues. It has all been about winning or losing, plus the insults and vitriol have made it impossible for the various parties to respect or trust one another in the future. To repeat one final time: The object of a negotiation should be to make a deal, not to prove your manhood!

❖   ❖   ❖   ❖   ❖

Even though he was not on the Taft Broadcasting Company's Board of Directors, Bernie Koteen was one of our most influential advisors, a wonderful friend, and the company's communications legal counsel. Bernie was the only Federal Communications lawyer Taft ever had, and we could not have done better. He was a superb lawyer and highly respected by the members of the Federal Communications Commission. Beyond all of that, he was an incredibly funny man. Three of his classics will make my point.

• One time we were involved in a complicated negotiation, and we decided to make a bold proposal that we hoped would conclude the deal. The proposal made us nervous because we were perhaps giving away more than we should, but we felt it might be the best way to get the deal done. After we had submitted our proposal, Bernie looked at me and said, "Charlie, our problem now is — can we afford to take yes for an answer!" I have never forgotten this line and have used it more than once since.

• On another occasion we were discussing the wisdom of guaranteeing a loan. Bernie had little regard for a guarantor. He said, "You know what a guarantor is? A schmuck with a pen."

- Finally, and perhaps most memorable, we were discussing someone with whom we were negotiating. Bernie had little respect for the wisdom and depth of this individual. He said, "Charlie, it's just sad, but down deep he's shallow."

A man who was completely obsessed with golf left the house before daybreak one Sunday, played all day and returned home just as night was descending. His irate wife met him at the door and said, "I just can't believe what you do, John. I think you love golf more than you love me." He thought a moment and replied, "you know, I think you're right. But, I love you more than tennis." (probably not a good idea to use this story in a group with many tennis players).

Here is a tip that you might use if the negotiations are going off track and/or the person you are dealing with is having trouble focusing on the issues. I have used this a few times and the results are always fascinating. You say to the person with whom you are negotiating, "You just put your finger on the heart of the matter." The other person will have no idea what you are talking about, but ashamed to admit it. Their mind is saying to them, "What heart? Which finger? What's he referring to?" This, then, gives you the perfect opportunity to spell out what you believe to be the heart of the matter, but which you attribute to him or her.

Brevity

I use this story to assure the audience that my remarks will be short. I find this to be helpful because the audience will relax a bit knowing that you will not be going on and on. Hopefully, it will remind you of the same intention!

I have come to the sad conclusion that at least 80 percent (this is my number and has absolutely no scientific basis) of all speeches, memoranda, and presentations — given anywhere in the world, at any given time — *are too long.* All of us should be sensitive to the length of what we are writing or saying. You will be amazed at how something can be pared down without limiting its meaning. Indeed, the meaning often becomes clearer when there is less verbiage to encumber it. I ran across a great story some years ago that went like this: A teacher asked a fourth-grade student to sum up the life of Socrates in four lines. Here's what the student said:

> Socrates lived long ago.
> He was very intelligent.
> Socrates gave long speeches.
> His friends poisoned him.

❖   ❖   ❖   ❖   ❖

Winston Churchill once said this about an overly long government report: "By its very length it defends itself against the risk of being read."

Complaining

A young man decided to become a monk. He entered a monastery and took the usual vow of silence. This particular order of monks had a very strict vow of silence. The young man was only allowed to say two words every seven years. At the end of the first seven years, he was brought before the senior monks and was told he could say his two words. "Bad food." he said. He returned to his cell. Seven years later, he was brought back in and asked for his two words. He looked his elders directly in the eye and said, "Cold floors." Back to his tiny cell. After seven more years, it was time again for his two words. In a clear, strong voice he said, "I quit." The elders looked at one another and one of them then said, "I'm not surprised. Ever since he got here, all he's done is complain."

❖   ❖   ❖   ❖   ❖

An embarrassing personal story — but a wonderful anecdote — happened when my parents, my brother, sister and I went to the Chicago World's Fair in 1933. Apparently, during our stay, I got very upset by something when we were out in a rowboat. My brother and sister took a picture of me standing up in the rowboat crying loudly but holding my fingers to my ears — presumably in the hope that I would not hear myself cry! Bill and Alice always said that, from that moment on, they were worried that I might not be the "brightest bulb in the chandelier." The lesson here is quite obvious; you can't conceal your anguish by simply plugging your ears!

❖   ❖   ❖   ❖   ❖

There is a wonderful story about the irrepressible and irreverent Alice Roosevelt Longworth. In her later years, she became a Grande Dame of Washington society and was known for her shocking and outrageous comments. My favorite is about a dinner party that she was hosting where she was seated on a couch in the living room of her home. When one of the guests arrived, she said, with a mischievous twinkle in her eye, "So nice to see you, dear." If you can't say something nice about anybody, sit here next to me.

❖   ❖   ❖   ❖   ❖

A wonderful epitaph summed up the thinking of the deceased buried there: "I told them I was sick!"

Conservatives & Liberals

The great comedian Mort Sahl defined a Conservative as one who believes that nothing should be done for the first time.

❖   ❖   ❖   ❖   ❖

When I was in law school, I spent one summer as a clerk in the office of the Attorney General of the state of Ohio. The Attorney General, C. William O'Neill, was a conservative Republican and, therefore, virtually all of the lawyers in the office were conservative — some quite conservative, at least by the standards of that day. We frequently had lunch together and almost always discussed politics in one form or another. One of the fellows in the group (I still remember his first name — Francis) was probably the most conservative of the group. He was constantly talking about the "liberals this" and "liberals that" and one day I stopped him and said, "Francis, what is your definition of a liberal?" He was virtually speechless. He had obviously never been asked this question before. Finally, he came out with this line, which I have never forgotten. "Well — uh — it means — uh — one of those people that believe in human rights." I can't say that I agree with this definition, but it was certainly the way he looked at things!

❖   ❖   ❖   ❖   ❖

Peter Wehner served in the last three Republican administrations. He wrote an op-ed piece in the "New York Times" on January 14, 2015. His final paragraph impressed me very much. Here's what he said: "Here's a good rule of thumb for politics: The stronger one's philosophical conservatisms are, the more important temperamental moderation becomes. Magnanimity, winsomeness and grace aren't antithetical to conservatism. They are an essential part of it."

I would only add that I think this is not just a good rule of thumb for politicians but for everyday life!

Courage & Risk Taking

This is one of my favorite anecdotes and I have used it often in situations where it is important to put an "act of courage" in perspective.

There was an oil well fire burning in Texas that was out of control. The fire that is, not Texas (but now that I think about it...). It had raged for days, and all efforts by all the great oil well firefighters from all over the world had failed. The fire continued to burn. The owners met to try to figure out what on earth they might do as they watched, literally, their fortune go up in smoke. Finally, one of the owners said, "There is one thing we haven't tried. Let's offer a $2 million reward for anyone who can put out the fire. A number of people came in to try, but failed. One day, the owners were standing on a high hill overlooking the valley in which the fire continued to burn. Suddenly, they heard a loud noise as an old dump truck raced by them heading right down the hill towards the fire. The driver appeared to be an old fellow in bib overalls and a straw hat, and the bed of the truck was a truly motley crew. To everyone's amazement, the truck drove right into the middle of the fire, and everyone in the truck began beating at the fire with blankets, seat covers, old burlap bags, and anything else they could get their hands on. Miraculously, in about five minutes the fire went out! The owners were, of course, overjoyed, and they ran down the hill to congratulate and thank the firefighters. When they got there the old fellow in the bib overalls was dusting off his clothes and straightening his hat when one of the owners said, "This is unbelievable. You have put out the fire. You are heroes. But even more important, you have won the $2 million reward. What do you intend to do with all that money?"

The old fellow thought a minute and then said, "I don't rightly know what I'll do with all of it, but the first thing I'm gonna do is buy brakes for that damned truck!" So, just remember: what might first look like courage is often nothing but a lack of brakes!

❖   ❖   ❖   ❖   ❖

It is interesting to speculate on what might have happened if the people involved in some of the great moments in history had lacked courage or been risk-averse. For example:

- Suppose Sir Edmund Hillary, as he and his sherpa neared the summit of Mt. Everest had said, "Tenzing, it's getting dark, it's really cold and I'm having trouble breathing. Let's go back down to the base camp and have a drink. We'll try this again tomorrow."

- Suppose Neil Armstrong had said to Buzz Aldrin, "You know, Buzz, we're running a little low on fuel. Maybe we better let somebody else be the first men on the moon."

- And, what if Wilbur Wright had said to Orville Wright, "It's awfully windy here and I'm not sure this crazy thing will fly anyway. Let's just forget it. We'll think of something simpler to invent — something that stays on the ground!"

- Obviously, you can make up your own examples and fit them to the audience or the occasion as appropriate.

❖   ❖   ❖   ❖   ❖

No one really cares if you can't dance well — just get up and dance!

❖   ❖   ❖   ❖   ❖

I liked to use this story when I wanted to emphasize the importance of "thinking outside the box."

This story concerns a company called Rainbow Crafts and its founder Joe McVicker. I was the company's lawyer early in my legal career. Rainbow Crafts owned and manufactured Play-Doh, the incredibly successful children's molding compound. Joe McVicker was a very impressive fellow, and he and I became good friends. I once asked him how he had come up with Play-Doh, and the story he told absolutely amazed me. Joe's brother-in-law ran a company, Kutol Products, that made wallpaper cleaner; Joe was also involved in this business. Most of those under fifty reading this book probably don't know what wallpaper cleaner was; it was a spongy-type substance containing a cleaning agent that was used to clean and brighten dirty or dusty wallpaper. Joe's sister ran a nursery school in the Washington, D. C, area, and she observed that if the wallpaper cleaner made by Kutol didn't have a cleaning agent in it, it would make a wonderful thing for the children in her nursery school to play with. Joe — and I assume his brother-in-law — figured out how to remove any harsh or toxic substances from the wallpaper cleaner and — it became Play-Doh! I'm sure it wasn't as simple as it sounds but many great ideas look simple in retrospect. As a kid, I helped my mother and dad more than once clean the wallpaper in our house using wallpaper cleaner. If I had only known the potential for the stuff I was holding in my hands! What I learned from Joe's story is that the essence of entrepreneurship — at least the American variety — is "to think outside the box" (my good friend W.R. Howell, former CEO of J. C. Penney, calls it "thinking the unthinkable") and always try to envision the greatest possible potential no matter how mundane the beginning may be. Joe McVicker was the classic example of American entrepreneurship at its best.

❖   ❖   ❖   ❖   ❖

Here is a wonderful follow-up to the Play-Doh story.

A young mechanical engineer, Richard James, was working for the Navy designing springs to support and stabilize instruments. In working with the springs, he made one walk off the counter and got a great idea. Four years later, the Slinky hit the market.

❖   ❖   ❖   ❖   ❖

Here's a story you can use to emphasize the importance of never betting against a "pro"

Kings Island is a world-class theme park located just north of Cincinnati. Taft Broadcasting Company built the park and opened it in 1972. Many exciting things have happened there over the years, but none more memorable than the famous Evel Knievel motorcycle jump over fourteen Greyhound buses in 1975. After Evel approached us to work with him on the jump, we decided it was a good idea for us because we knew it would draw large crowds and give national publicity to Kings Island. So the deal was arranged. Evel came to town and spent a week or so before the jump getting ready. One day, after I'd gotten to know him fairly well, he said he wanted to play some golf. (He was a very good golfer.) I agreed and suggested that we play at our Jack Nicklaus course right across the highway from Kings Island. Evel thought that was fine and we agreed to meet the next morning. That night I was speaking to a friend and told him that I planned to play with Evel the next morning. He warned me that Evel would bet on almost anything, and he added, "His bets are not small!" The following morning, the course was a little sloppy because it had rained during the night. But, it was playable and so we teed it up and were on our way. After decent drives on the first hole, each of our second shots into the green plugged in mud in front of the green — four or five yards short of the putting surface. As we walked toward the green, Evel turned to me and said,

"I'll bet you a thousand dollars that my ball has more mud on it than yours." I was speechless, but managed finally to say, "Evel, I'm not a betting man, and I'm certainly not a good enough golfer to bet you. Let's just have fun today." We did have fun and I kept my wallet in my pocket. By the way, Evel went on to make the bus-jump on national television in front of some twenty-five thousand people. He was an incredible guy, and I'll never forget the time we spent together.

❖   ❖   ❖   ❖   ❖

This is a great story to highlight that sometimes the majority does not rule and that — sometimes — that's a good thing.

Over the years, Ted Gregory and I became very good friends. Ted was the legendary "Ribs King" whose Montgomery Inn ribs became — and remain — world famous. I would see him whenever we went to his restaurant (in Montgomery, a suburb of Cincinnati) and I also ran into him frequently in downtown Cincinnati. Although I have scores of happy memories of times with Ted, my favorite has to do with his plan to build another restaurant on the Ohio riverfront. He told me some of his family were very skeptical of the project and were understandably nervous that it would not be successful, given all the competition it would face. Ted was concerned that he would not be able to persuade them that it was the right thing to do. Some weeks later, I ran into him again and asked about the status of the project. He smiled and said that it was going forward. I told him how pleased I was and wondered how he had overcome the family's concerns. His answer was one I never forgot. He said, "I decided to have a family meeting. The vote was 8 to 1 against building the restaurant. But, I was the 1 — so we're gonna do it!" As usual, Ted was right on the money. The restaurant has been a huge success. One final note about the Gregorys: Mattie, Ted's wife, was as understated as Ted was over stated. She was obviously his anchor and played a very important role in the success of their businesses. I'm sure Ted would be the first one to point out that he was a very lucky guy to have married Mattie!

❖   ❖   ❖   ❖   ❖

This is a great story to illustrate the importance of having the courage to do something that most people would think foolish or at least unnecessary.

Another great innovator that I was privileged to know was Paul Smucker, the longtime CEO of the J. M. Smucker Company. Of the many things that Paul did to grow the Smucker Company, I think one of the most important was when he agreed with the company's advertising agency to adopt the now-famous slogan "With a name like Smucker's, it has to be good." Believe me, a lot of people in Paul's position would have rejected the idea of making fun of the family name. Paul saw it quite differently — and was he ever right! It has become one of the great tag lines in the history of American business. There is an interesting backstory to Paul's decision. His son Richard told me that before making the final decision, Paul called a small meeting of major family members and explained to them the slogan that had been proposed. He pointed out that he didn't want to go ahead with this (inasmuch as it made light of the family name) without the group's agreement. As Richard tells the story, one of the older members of the family asked Paul whether he felt the slogan might help business and lead to higher dividends. When he said he thought it might, she said, "Count me in!"

❖   ❖   ❖   ❖   ❖

If you conclude that somebody doesn't have the courage to deal with a particular problem, just remember what a wise man once said, "No problem is too great or complex that it can't be walked away from."

Dealing with Adversity

One of my favorite lines is, "If you can smile in the face of adversity, it's because you've found someone to blame"

❖   ❖   ❖   ❖   ❖

A similar comment described a "colleague" as someone who is called in at the last minute to share the blame.

❖   ❖   ❖   ❖   ❖

When dealing with difficult situations, it is critical that you not do things that make the situation even worse than it is. As someone put it, "If you find yourself in a hole, the first thing to do is to stop digging."

❖   ❖   ❖   ❖   ❖

Perhaps the most important thing in dealing with adversity is to never give up. Here is a great take on a Latin phrase *Non illegitimi carborundum est*. The loose translation is "Don't let the bastards grind you down."

❖   ❖   ❖   ❖   ❖

Here is a wonderful story from the incomparable *New Yorker* writer, A.J. Liebling. It appeared in the August 3, 1940 issue of the *New Yorker*. This was a time when Liebling was covering the deteriorating situation in wartime Paris. Here's what he said: "Two kinds of persons are consoling in a dangerous time. Those who are completely courageous and those who are more frightened than you are."

❖   ❖   ❖   ❖   ❖

A custom grew at Taft Broadcasting Company which led to a lot of laughs and fun. I had heard a joke about a mythical bird called the Foo bird. The joke goes like this.

A wealthy explorer and bird watcher felt that he had seen and catalogued virtually every bird in the world except one — the Foo bird. In doing some research, he learned that the bird was virtually extinct and survived only in a very remote area in central Africa. Determined to find it he made his way to a tiny village in the area where the bird had last been sighted. He met with the tribal elders who confirmed that the bird was occasionally seen but warned him of a legend that had been part of the Foo bird lore forever. They told him that if he spotted the Foo bird he needed to be very careful because if the bird "droppings" touched his skin and he wiped it off he would immediately die. Appropriately forewarned — but very skeptical — he headed into the bush. The day was hot and long and in the late afternoon, as he was about to give up, he suddenly spotted in the sky above what, without question, was a Foo bird. Joyously, he ran after the bird and took as many photographs as he could when suddenly the bird "deposited" right on his arm and then flew away. He instinctively took out his handkerchief and started to rub off the "deposit" because, with the heat of the day and the sweat on his body, the stench was already beginning. However, at the last moment, he remembered the warning of the tribal elders and put his handkerchief away, feeling a little bit foolish but also a little bit frightened. As he made his way back to his camp, the smell of the "droppings" became intolerable and his arm began to throb and itch. He couldn't stand it any longer and pulled out his handkerchief and wiped off the unpleasant dropping. Immediately he collapsed and died. There is a very important moral to this story. It is simply this. "If the Foo shits, wear it."

❖   ❖   ❖   ❖   ❖

I have never found a story that I felt better illustrated dealing with adversity than this: Had the hunter continued to look adversity in the face, he would still be alive!

Ego

I'm sure in your life, as in mine, you have heard people suggest or imply that they are irreplaceable in a particular job or calling. Here is the perfect response:

Just remember the cemeteries are filled with indispensable people.

❖   ❖   ❖   ❖   ❖

If you think you're a big deal, try ordering somebody else's dog around or, even better, try to train a cat to do tricks.

❖   ❖   ❖   ❖   ❖

An old country song put it this way, "If I ain't got it, you don't need it."

❖   ❖   ❖   ❖   ❖

An ancient Italian proverb says it well: Just remember, after the chess match, the king and the pawn go in the same box.

❖   ❖   ❖   ❖   ❖

Don't try this story in Texas. But, it works great everywhere else!

A "big deal" rancher from Texas was traveling through the country-side of Vermont when he spotted an old farmer plowing his field near the road. He stopped his car, walked over, and introduced himself. He then said to the old farmer, "How big of a spread have you got here, old man?" The farmer, in a classic clipped Vermont twang said, "'bout seventy acres." The rancher replied, "Do you know that at my ranch in Texas I can get up in the morning, get in my car, and drive all day, and still not be at the other end of my land? Whadaya think of that?" The Vermont farmer thought a minute, smiled and said, "That so? I had a car like that once!"

❖   ❖   ❖   ❖   ❖

You might also try this old saying — "If you can't beat 'em, just say they didn't do it."

❖   ❖   ❖   ❖   ❖

A middle-aged woman had a heart attack and was taken to the hospital. On the operating table, she had a near-death experience and had a conversation with God. She asked God if it was the end for her. God said no, explaining she would recover and live for another thirty or forty years. Upon her recovery, the woman decided, seeing as though she was going to live so long, that she might as well stay in the hospital and have a facelift, liposuction, breast augmentation and a tummy tuck. Walking away from the hospital after all the nips and tucks, she was struck by an ambulance and killed. In heaven, she asked God: "I thought you said I was to live another thirty or forty years?' God replied: "Sorry, I didn't recognize you."

Enemies

"I have never killed a man, but I have read many obituaries with great pleasure." — *Clarence Darrow*

❖   ❖   ❖   ❖   ❖

"I didn't attend the funeral, but I sent a nice letter that I approved of it." — *Mark Twain*

❖   ❖   ❖   ❖   ❖

"I just learned about his illness. Let's hope it's nothing trivial." – *Irwin S. Cobb*

❖   ❖   ❖   ❖   ❖

Al Hrabosky, a former major league relief pitcher, had a marvelous comment on how to react to your enemies. He said, "When I'm on the road my greatest ambition is to get a standing boo."

❖   ❖   ❖   ❖   ❖

Pogo, a comic strip created by Walt Kelly, was rich with satire and social commentary, much like "Doonesbury" for its time. Pogo's great line has become a classic. "We have met the enemy and he is us." Another great line which seems strangely appropriate to some of our nation's current challenges: Pogo said, "Declare a victory and retreat!"

Environment

Here's a slogan that I love: "Save the earth. It's the only planet with chocolate."

❖   ❖   ❖   ❖   ❖

The four food groups are: Fast, Frozen, Instant, Chocolate.

❖   ❖   ❖   ❖   ❖

We have all become quite used to "smoking" and "non-smoking"" areas. What some of the younger readers of this book may not know is that, in the beginning, there were some actions in this regard which now seem almost unbelievable. For example, there was a smoking and a non-smoking section in certain airlines, seemingly totally disregarding the impossibility of keeping smoke confined in an enclosed area. This reminded me of an early experience that I had on a Board of Directors on which I served as a young man. There were probably 20 people on the Board, at least six or eight of whom smoked cigars. When a few of the non-cigar smokers suggested to the Chairman (himself a cigar smoker) that the air quality was something other than perfect, his response was to put all of the cigar smokers at one end of the table! Eventually, when the futility of this became apparent, the cigar smokers were asked to refrain during the meeting. Though there was much loud grumbling, they agreed.

Experts

I have used this story countless times. It works best at the beginning of your remarks when you are trying to establish that self-proclaimed "experts" should be viewed as suspect.

There was a renowned chemistry professor who was out on his annual lecture tour. He went from campus to campus discoursing on his field of expertise. To help him with the mechanics of the trip was his long time, loyal chauffeur. The professor always gave the same lecture at the various stops, and towards the end of the tour, both he and his chauffeur were getting a little weary of the whole exercise. As they approached the site of the last lecture, the chauffeur said, "You know, let's have a little fun tonight. I know your lecture by heart. I've heard it thirty-eight times. I'd like to deliver it." To which the professor said, "Sounds like a wonderful idea. You do that. I'll put on your chauffeur's uniform. I'll sit in the back of the audience and pretend to be you. It will be great." The chauffeur did a marvelous job of giving the speech and no one was the wiser. When the speech was over, there was a great round of applause. The chauffeur nodded modestly and was about to retire, when from the audience came, "Question, question." Well, of course, all lectures are followed by Q & A, so the chauffeur looked at the raised hand and said, "By all means, go ahead." The question was from a chemistry professor at the university. He said, "What is the co-efficient of plutonium times the valence of copper as a factor of stress in the early curve of nuclear fission development when the reactor is lead based?" Well, the chauffeur didn't miss a beat. He said, "Sir, I recognize you from photographs that I've seen in trade journals, and I know you are very renowned and respected. But I must say that I'm astounded that a man of your reputation could ask such a question. Why, my chauffeur in the back of the room can answer that!"

❖   ❖   ❖   ❖   ❖

Here's a short and sweet definition of an expert:

The definition of an EXPERT: A bull-shitter from out-of-town.

Forecasting the Future

This story works well when you are trying to make the point that looking long-range is fine, but that one should never forget the "short" range.

Many years ago, I was attending a conference in Cleveland, Ohio, during which we heard a speech from the much-acclaimed business leader and visionary Dr. Simon Ramo. One of my good friends, Don Hinckley, CEO of Emery Industries, Inc., one of Cincinnati's finest companies, was also in the audience. It is important before going on to note that the speech was given in September. Dr. Ramo gave a superb, thought-provoking talk and shared his vision for coming decades and even longer. When he finished, he asked for questions. My friend Don raised his hand and said, "Dr. Ramo, I have truly enjoyed your vision of the future. But let me ask you this. How do you see October?" Don's question brought down the house, and Dr. Ramo shared the laughs.

❖   ❖   ❖   ❖   ❖

Over forty years ago, one of the nation's biggest airlines announced that it would be the first to take people to the moon. This seemed fitting in view of its strength and stature at the time. Guess what airline it was? Pan Am!

❖   ❖   ❖   ❖   ❖

When the Yankees signed Babe Ruth in 1930 to a two-year contract worth $160,000, General Manager Ed Barrow proudly exclaimed, "No one will ever be paid more."

Forecasting the future is obviously tricky business. Certain things that you think will be around forever sometimes vanish without a trace. Just consider videotape, movie rental stores, dial-up internet, the evening news, and 8-track tapes.

The world will miss the great Yogi Berra. His contributions to the English language are legendary. Consider this quote as it pertains to forecasting the future: "If you don't know where you are going, you're liable to end up somewhere else."

Fragility of Language

It is so easy to say something that seems clear but carries a double meaning quite different than the one you intend.

Many years ago, my brother, who was a minister, sent me a number of excerpts from church bulletins that vividly — and amusingly — illustrate my point. Here are a few:

- The associate minister unveiled the church's new tithing campaign slogan last Sunday: "I upped my pledge — up yours."

- This being Easter Sunday, we will ask Mrs. Lewis to come forward and lay an egg on the altar.

- Irvin Benson and Jessie Carter were married on October 24 in the church. So ends a friendship that began in their school days.

- And my personal favorite: The Low Self-Esteem Group will meet Thursday at 7:00 p.m. in the Social Hall. Please use the back door.

- The sermon this morning is "Jesus Walks on the Water." The sermon tonight is "Searching for Jesus."

- Miss Charlene Mason sang "I Will Not Pass This Way Again," giving obvious pleasure to the congregation.

- Barbara remains in the hospital and needs blood donors for more transfusions. She is also having trouble sleeping and requests tapes of Pastor Jack's sermons.

The Washington Post has for many years challenged its readers in the so called "Mensa Invitational." The object is to invite readers to take one word from the dictionary, alter it by adding or subtracting or changing one letter and then supplying a new definition. Some of the entries are hilarious. For example:

- Intaxication: Euphoria at getting a tax refund — it lasts until you realize it was your money to start with.

- Giraffiti: Vandalism spray painted very, very high.

- Karmageddon: it's like, when everybody is sending off all these really bad vibes, right? And then, like, the earth explodes and it's, like, a serious bummer.

- Decafalon: The grueling event of getting through the day consuming only things that are good for you.

The point of this is clear. Language is very fragile. It is extremely important in making any sort of presentation that you make sure that the words say what you mean them to say.

There is a wonderful story about the great British statesman Benjamin Disraeli, who said, when asked to define the difference between a misfortune and a calamity, "If Mr. Gladstone [his principal adversary] fell into the Thames, that would be a misfortune. If someone pulled him out, that would be a calamity." It's a great line.

❖   ❖   ❖   ❖   ❖

Perhaps my favorite story that illustrates the fragility of language is one that happened during my Taft Broadcasting Company days. I mentioned earlier one of Taft Broadcasting Company's theme parks, Canada's Wonderland,. Periodically, several of us would travel to the park for business meetings. The park had a great chef who would always feed us a wonderful lunch before we headed back to Cincinnati. One day, after an ample meal, he brought out a large plate of chocolate éclairs. We said we were too full to eat another bite, but the éclairs looked so good that we asked him if we could take them back with us. Now, the rest of the story.

As we were flying back in our company airplane, one of my associates raised a concern. He pointed out that we might have trouble clearing customs with food being brought on the plane from outside the country. We acknowledged that this was a real problem and decided to hide the box behind one of the seats. We always flew into a small private airport near Cincinnati and we knew most of the custom agents. We did not expect that the agent would make a search of the airplane. We landed and taxied up to the customs location. The agent came out of his office and we opened the door of the plane to let him in. Of course, we were not allowed to disembark until after we had been cleared. The agent mounted the steps, stuck his head into the plane, and said, "Do you have anything to declare?" The problem was that what he said sounded very much like, "Do you have anything to éclair?" We, of course, broke into a fit of laughter. He responded with, "What's so funny?" We told him that we wanted to throw ourselves on the mercy of the court and admitted that we were hiding a treasure trove of luscious chocolate éclairs. He joined in the laughter, then we all had an éclair and headed for home.

Getting Ahead

A crow was sitting in a tree, doing nothing all day. A rabbit came along and asked him, "Can I also sit like you and do nothing all day long?" The crow answered, "Sure, why not?" So, the rabbit sat on the ground below the crow and rested. A fox jumped on the rabbit and ate it. Moral of the story: To be sitting and doing nothing, you must be sitting very high up!

❖   ❖   ❖   ❖   ❖

A turkey was chatting with a bull. "I would love to be able to get to the top of that tree," sighed the turkey, "but I haven't got the energy." "Well, why don't you nibble on my droppings?" replied the bull, "they're packed with nutrients." The turkey pecked at a lump of dung and found that it gave him enough strength to reach the lowest branch of the tree. The next day, after eating some more dung, he reached the second branch. Finally, after a fourth night, there he was proudly perched at the top of the tree. Soon he was spotted by a farmer, who shot the turkey out of the tree. Moral of the story: Bullshit might get you to the top, but it won't keep you there.

Glibness

There is no credible evidence that the tongue is connected to the brain.

❖   ❖   ❖   ❖   ❖

He manages like a balloonist. He thinks hot air will take him a long way.

❖   ❖   ❖   ❖   ❖

I wish I knew who came up with this because it is brilliant. It is especially valuable for young people who live with this vocabulary every day.

The tendency to be glib and to use big words and current "jargon" is exacerbated by the world that we currently live in. First of all, technology causes big words to be used less frequently. There isn't space for long words in a text or a tweet. As Elizabeth Bernstein has noted in a very interesting article in *The Wall Street Journal*, "We're communicating across so many different channels, by such necessity, our language is becoming abbreviated." Let me illustrate this by reproducing something called "Bullshit Bingo." It is one of the funniest things I have run across with respect to using current catch words and phrases. I can't describe it adequately so I am reproducing it here. I have no idea who dreamed it up but they deserve a Nobel Prize for humor, if there were such a prize — and I really wish there were!

Do you keep falling asleep in meetings and seminars? What about those long and boring conference calls? Here is a way to change all of that!

How to play: Check off each block when you hear these words during a meeting, seminar, or phone call. When you get five blocks horizontally, vertically, or diagonally, YOU WIN!!

Synergy	Strategic Fit	Core Competencies	Best Practice	Bottom Line
Revisit	Take that Offline	24/7	Out of the Loop	Benchmark
Value-Added	Proactive	Win-Win	Think Outside The Box	Fast Track
Result-Driven	Empower [or] Empower-ment	Knowledge Base	At the End of the Day	Touch Base
Mindset	Client Focus[ed]	Ball Park	Game Plan	Leverage

Some other words that would fit right into this game are:
1. Robust 2. Suite 3. Closure 4. Edgy 5. Brand

Good News, Bad News

This story works well with any audience, but especially with an audience that includes some golfers. By the way, it is a story that could be changed so as to reference another sport. For example: The good news might be "I bowled a 300-game yesterday."

The dentist completes his annual check-up and says, "I have good news and bad news — which do you want first?" The patient responds, "Well, let's get the bad news out of the way." The dentist replied, "You have some very serious dental problems. You need two root canals and they will be expensive and difficult. But you must have them done." The man was obviously not happy, so he said, "Well then, let's hear the good news. The dentist smiled and said, "I had a hole in one yesterday."

❖   ❖   ❖   ❖   ❖

The definition of mixed emotions is having your 18-year-old daughter arrive home at 7:30 a.m. with a Gideon Bible under her arm.

Gullibility

We sometimes fall for something we don't truly comprehend for fear of being left out of something we are sure everybody else understands. A classic example of this is the full-page ad that supposedly ran in a major metropolitan newspaper some years ago that said simply, "Last Day to Send in Your Dollar" and then listed a P.O. Box to which the money should be sent. Apparently, thousands of dollars came flooding in from people who obviously had no idea what they were doing but didn't want to be left out.

❖   ❖   ❖   ❖   ❖

Don't ever forget the famous P. T. Barnum quote: "There's a sucker born every minute."

Hard Work

Over the years, I have often made a speech that I call "Ingredients of Success." The first ingredient that I mention is hard work. It is always interesting to see the reaction of the audience. More often than not, a wide-eyed look that suggests that the listeners had really never thought of hard work as an important part of success. The following anecdotes are designed to deal with that issue.

A man prayed and asked God to help him win the lottery. Every day he renewed his prayer and finally said, "God, won't you please help me win the lottery?" To his absolute amazement the skies darkened, lighting flashed and a strong deep voice said, "Would you at least buy a ticket." We so often expect good things to happen without effort. They rarely do.

❖　　❖　　❖　　❖　　❖

To put it another way: Any time the going gets easy, you'd better check and see if you are going downhill.

❖　　❖　　❖　　❖　　❖

I once dreamed up an acronym — TANSTAAFL — to underscore the importance of hard work in achieving any level of success. The acronym stands for There Ain't No Such Thing As A Free Lunch.

❖   ❖   ❖   ❖   ❖

Leave it to Yogi Berra to have the best comment. Yogi said, "Give 100% to everything you do and if that isn't enough, give everything you have left."

❖   ❖   ❖   ❖   ❖

I learned two very important lessons during the four summers that I spent working on a county highway road crew. First, I was young and looking to the future. But for most of the guys I worked with, this was their life. This is how they supported themselves and their families. For most of them, this was their future. It gave me a new and different perspective on the lives and dreams of what, I suspect, was the vast majority of people at that time — and now, for that matter.

❖   ❖   ❖   ❖   ❖

The other lesson I learned came from an old guy who was very friendly to me from the very beginning. His name was Emmett, and he had been part of the crew for years. He was an intelligent, pleasant man and very popular with all of us. He and I were working together one day to dig a trench for some pipe. He watched me stabbing furiously at the ground with my shovel; he stopped me and showed me how to shovel slowly and carefully. He was obviously proud of the fact that he could do something well and that he could pass this knowledge on to someone else. This may seem a trivial incident, but it had a real effect on me, then and now. No matter how menial a task may seem, it can be done well or it can be done badly; it can be done with pride or with resentment; it can be done with total effort or with disdain. I think that lesson applies — or should apply — to any task that anyone ever undertakes. It's funny how and where you learn important lessons!

Honesty

Trust in the Lord — but lock your car!

❖   ❖   ❖   ❖   ❖

One of the greatest lines about honesty that I ever heard: "Never buy anything from someone who is out of breath."

❖   ❖   ❖   ❖   ❖

Never believe anything until it has been officially denied at the highest level.

❖   ❖   ❖   ❖   ❖

Another unforgettable quote from Groucho Marx: "Those are my principles, and if you don't like them. I have others."

❖   ❖   ❖   ❖   ❖

One of my good friends offered this very sage advice: "Always tell the truth. There are several reasons to do this, including that the truth is much easier to remember."

❖   ❖   ❖   ❖   ❖

The next two stories are from popular comic strips. When I use these stories I often point out that wisdom can be found in unusual places — like the "funny papers."

A truly great Peanuts comic strip has Lucy as the psychiatrist consulting with Charlie Brown. Her question to him is, "Which do you prefer, a sunrise or a sunset?" When he answers, "A sunset, I guess." Lucy launches into a diatribe. She points out that people who prefer sunsets always give up, they always move back instead of forward and she just knew that he wouldn't prefer a "sunrise" because those are for people with ambition. Therefore, she concludes that Charlie Brown is hopeless. In the final frame, Charlie looks wistfully at the reader and says, "Actually, I've always sort of preferred noon!"

Some years ago, there was a very amusing (at least to me) B.C. comic strip about golf. Every golfer should ponder the message. In the first panel B. C. was explaining golf to his girlfriend, saying, "The object is to hit the ball as few times as possible. In the second panel, his girlfriend repeats, with some puzzlement, "So the object of the game is to hit the ball as few times as possible?" He responds, "Yes." She says, "Then why hit it at all?" and walks away. In the final panel, B. C. is sitting alone in the dark staring at the moon repeating in almost a dazed way, "Then, why hit it at all?"

Paul Harvey, the great radio personality, once said, "Golf is a game in which you yell 'fore', shoot six and write down five."

Humility

This is a story that can most effectively be used after you have received a flattering introduction.

It's important to keep flattery and nice words in perspective. A man was once introduced to a large gathering as a very successful businessman who had made a million dollars in California oil. He arose, somewhat flustered and said that, although he didn't want to embarrass the introducer, he did want to be honest. Although the facts, he said, were essentially correct, he felt compelled to clarify that the state wasn't California, it was Pennsylvania; it wasn't oil, it was coal; it wasn't a million dollars, it was a hundred thousand; it wasn't him, it was his brother; and he didn't make it, he lost it!

❖   ❖   ❖   ❖   ❖

If you are unable to keep flattery and praise from turning your head, you can rely on your family to keep your ego under control. A good example is the following story. A wife read the fortune telling card that her husband got from a penny weighing machine. "You are a leader," she read, "with a magnetic personality and strong character — intelligent, witty, and attractive." Then she turned the card over and added, "It's got your weight wrong, too!"

❖   ❖   ❖   ❖   ❖

You obviously need to be careful when using a tragic event to make a point in a humorous way. This story proves that it can be done if enough time has lapsed and if the story does not trivialize the disaster itself.

One of the great national disasters was the Johnstown flood of 1889. The scale of the flood was hard to imagine. The wreckage of a dam brought forth a torrent of twenty million tons of water. The flood killed over 2,200 people and caused many millions of dollars of damage.

One of the residents — and survivors — of the flood was an old gentleman who made a "career" of talking about the great flood. He would talk to anyone who would listen and sometimes to those who didn't listen. It became a consuming passion of his life. When he passed away and went to heaven he had his interview with St. Peter, who asked him if there was anything about his life that he wished to mention. The old gentleman said that he was a survivor of the Johnstown flood and knew more about it than anyone. He bragged that he had made many speeches about it. St. Peter replied that he thought this would be a very interesting subject for the folks in heaven to hear about. The old man was notably excited and was effusive in his thanks. St. Peter then said, "But there is one thing you should know before you make your speech." "What could that be?" asked the old man. St. Peter responded, "Noah will probably be in the audience."

❖　❖　❖　❖　❖

A friend of mine from the University of Minnesota passed on the following quote. I find it very moving and a marvelous expression of the true essence of humility. "A civilization flourishes when its people plant trees under which they will never sit."

❖　❖　❖　❖　❖

When you're trying to make the point that life has its ups and downs, you should recall that some days you're the pigeon, and some days you're the statue.

Intelligence

One of the most interesting comments on intelligence that I have ever heard came from a former law partner of mine, a distinguished litigator. He was involved in a lawsuit in which he took the deposition of a very prominent gentleman who was internationally known and often praised for his intelligence. After the deposition, I asked my friend his opinion of this celebrated individual. He said simply, "He's the dumbest smart man I ever met." This phrase is worth thinking about. Without common sense and good judgment, "intelligence" in the classic sense is not worth much.

❖   ❖   ❖   ❖   ❖

Albert Einstein had little use for rote learning. Instead, his creative genius stemmed from his ability to imagine concepts. He summed this up by once stating, "Imagination is more important than knowledge."

Marketing

One of the greatest statements that I have ever seen on the subject of marketing came in a speech by Ed Harness, the CEO of Procter and Gamble, in addressing the annual marketing meeting of the Conference Board in New York City a number of years ago. Here are a couple of excerpts from Ed's speech.

- The key to successful marketing is superior product performance.

- While advertising and selling are certainly important, we have never been able to build a successful brand through these skills alone. Advertising and selling skills can get consumers to try the product but after that the health of the brand depends entirely on satisfaction with its performance.

- Advertising has no life of its own. It has no unique power to persuade. It is simply a part of a total marketing process which, to be successful, must be based on a worthwhile product.

❖   ❖   ❖   ❖   ❖

The president of a dog food company was addressing the annual sales meeting of his company. He was not happy. Sales were poor and he was giving the group a stern lecture. He said, "I simply don't understand it. We have the finest product in the business, our packaging and marketing are second to none. yet sales are terrible. You guys must not be doing your job. Just tell me what's wrong." There were several seconds of silence until one guy in the back of the room raised his hand. The president said, "Okay, so you think you know what's wrong? Then tell me." The fellow, in a frightened voice said, "Sir, the problem is that the dogs don't like it."

❖   ❖   ❖   ❖   ❖

In marketing, it is always critical to really understand where the strength of your product truly resides. Here is what one observer described as the key to the movie business. He said, "Find a good popcorn location and build a theater around it."

❖   ❖   ❖   ❖   ❖

Two old fellows who had tried their hand unsuccessfully in a variety of businesses, decided to try selling cantaloupes from the back of their truck along the highway. Things were not going well and they decided to try to figure out what went wrong and what to do about it.

The one fellow said to the other, "How much are we paying for the cantaloupe?" The other fellow answered, "We're paying a dollar a cantaloupe." The first fellow responds, "Well, then, what are we selling 'em for?" "We're selling 'em for ninety cents a cantaloupe," came the answer. The first fellow thought about the situation for a moment and then said, "Well, I think I've got the answer. We've got to get a bigger truck."

Sadly, this thought process enters into business decisions and strategies more than you might think.

❖   ❖   ❖   ❖   ❖

This is a classic case of putting your best foot forward in your sales pitch.

In marketing a new garbage collection service, the owner used the following pitch: "If you are not satisfied, double your trash back."

Maturity/ Growing Up

You have reached maturity on the day that you realize that there is someone else who is better than you at what you do best. If you have not already had this experience, you will. And, if you have had the experience you will know precisely what I mean.

Someone said that age is a very high price to pay for maturity.

❖   ❖   ❖   ❖   ❖

This is a story from my early days as a lawyer. I use it to underscore the importance of experience and maturity. It also illustrates how a tragic event in one's past stays with one forever.

A young German immigrant named Ewald Pawsat came to the United States and settled first in Sheboygan, Wisconsin, then moved to Maysville, Kentucky where he started Wald, a bicycle repair shop. Over the years, he built the company into the largest supplier of bicycle parts made in the United States, selling to all the big bicycle manufacturers. The law firm that I was with represented Mr. Pawsat, and I was asked to work on his estate plan. After many meetings, his will was finally ready for signature. I met him at his office in Maysville to take care of the signing. But before that, I told him that I wanted to be sure that he had disclosed all matters of significance regarding his holdings, because if he had not I could not be sure that the will was what it should be. Mr. Pawsat by this time was in his seventies and was a man of enormous integrity. He said to me, "Well, there is one thing that I have not told you about." When I asked what he meant, he explained that he was keeping some cash in the safe in his office that he had not mentioned to me. I assumed he was talking about a few thousand dollars. So I said, "Well, I don't see that as a problem — how much are we talking about?" He paused and said, "Around $300,000." This was in the mid-1960s! I swallowed hard and said, "Sir, I really think that's too much money to be keeping in your safe. You should have it working for you at a bank or whatever." At this point his voice got stronger and he said, "Let me explain something to you, young man. There was a time during the Great Depression when the banks closed and I was unable to raise enough cash to pay my employees, and that lasted for a whole two-week pay period. That was the most embarrassing thing that I had ever experienced, and I vowed that I would never let it happen again. $300,000 is the amount I would need to meet a payroll, and there is nothing that you or anybody else can say to make me take it out of that safe."

That comment has never really left my mind. Another lesson learned: Those who went through the Great Depression, including my own father, never really recovered from it in terms of their trust in the stability of our system

Meetings

A plaque in my office beautifully sums up my attitude regarding meetings. It reads:

> "Any simple problem can be made insoluble
> if enough meetings are held to discuss it."

❖　　❖　　❖　　❖　　❖

"If you had to identify, in one word, the reason why the human race has not achieved, and never well achieve, its full potential, that word would be meetings." — *Dave Barry*

❖　　❖　　❖　　❖　　❖

Although this story is perhaps too long for you to use in its entirety, it is so good I wanted to share it all. You can, hopefully, pick out the parts that best fits the situation you are addressing.

Some years ago, *The Wall Street Journal* carried an article quoting a man named Craig Wright, then the Manager of Medical and Health Services for the Xerox Corporation. He wrote about the stress on executives caused by the amount of time they lost in meetings. He did it in a very unusual way — a biblical way — but one that makes the point vividly.

"And as the conclaves multiplied and lapped one upon another, they were delayed in starting and delayed in ending, and were postponed to be called again when those whose presence was required could be made free. For the message was clear, but the ways were hidden.

Then from all sides came voices crying out —

'Though I labour from my coming in to my going out.
I cannot attend the meetings for which I am summoned.'
'It concerned me not, yet was I called unto meeting.'
'My need for decision is great, yet am I denied, for all are in meetings.'
'Can the meeting not start by the mark on the glass?'
'To the meeting for which I made ready, no person came.'
'Is thy servant a fool, that thou summonest him to a meeting to schedule meetings?'

I. Thou shalt not meet if the matter can be resolved by other means.

II. Thou shalt make the purpose of each meeting known to those thou summonest.

III. Thou shall summon only those whose presence is needful.

IV. Thou shalt start at the time announced.

V. Thou shalt stop when it is meet and right so to do.

VI. Thou shalt not run beyond.

VII. Thou shouldst combine into one those which need not be separate.

VIII. Prepare thy thoughts, that the minutes not be wasted.

IX. Schedule not in haste, for the day is short in which to do that which thou hast to do.

X. Fear not to cancel if need disappears.

Permit me a postscript to this section. I know that it is a bit of a digression, but I am not sure I will ever write another book and I have some thoughts regarding meetings that I am anxious to share. These are observations that I have accumulated as a result of the literally thousands of meetings that I have been part of over the years. Here they are. It is interesting to note that many of these observations are similar to the ones mentioned in The Wall Street Journal *article on page 62.*

1. Never schedule a meeting unless there is a strong and compelling reason to do so.
2. Meetings to plan later meetings are to be avoided at all costs.
3. Make clear that what I think of as "attention-diverting devices" are checked at the door. This includes laptops, cell phones, and miscellaneous other devices that I probably don't even know exist.
4. Prepare and send out an agenda in advance.
5. At the end of the meeting, it is critical to agree on next steps and who is responsible for each.
6. If you are meeting with a group for the first time — you should talk little and listen much.
7. If you are among the most junior in the meeting, respect your elders.
8. If you are among the seniors in the meeting don't pontificate or be condescending in an effort to prove how wise you are.
9. Whether you are junior, senior or somewhere in between — be brief!
10. Hold your temper. It is so easy when things become contentious to lose one's temper. It is the biggest mistake you can make.
11. Just as you should hold your temper, you should also CURB YOUR ENTHUSIASM.
12. BE ON TIME. Punctuality is a great virtue.

❖   ❖   ❖   ❖   ❖

Never judge any participant in a meeting based on your initial impression. Here an anecdote is appropriate.

I had a classic example of this in my early days as a lawyer. I was asked to serve on the board of a hospital in Cincinnati. I went to my first board meeting and noted with interest that one of the greatest businessmen in Cincinnati and, indeed, in America was on the board. He was in his eighties, but remained a business legend. It was a luncheon meeting and I couldn't help but notice a severe tremor in his hands and arms. As he struggled with the meal, I remember thinking how sad it was that this great mind could no longer deal with the issues that we would be discussing. Boy, was I wrong! Indeed, as a wonderful German Law Professor once said in one of my classes in law school, "Herr Mechem, you couldn't be wronger." When the meal was over and we addressed the business of the meeting, especially the financial statements, this old gentleman proved why he had become such a legend. He cut through the financial information like a knife through butter. He was smarter, by far, than anyone else in the room.

❖   ❖   ❖   ❖   ❖

A dear friend of mine, Bob Wehling recounts this experience. While he was serving as Advertising Manager of the Soap Division of Procter & Gamble he went to his first meeting with the head of Product Development. When he walked into the meeting room and before he could say a ward, the head of Product Development welcomed him and said, "The purpose of this meeting is for you to agree with my point of view." As Bob observed, we have both been in many meetings with people who thought that way, but this was the only time he had actually heard someone say it!

Men and Women

I can't remember the author of this line but he or she should have been proud to say it — "Women who seek to be the equal of men are not setting their sights high enough."

❖ ❖ ❖ ❖ ❖

There has been much talk in recent years of a "glass ceiling" prohibiting women from advancing. This is a fanciful description. A better one is "There is no glass ceiling — only a thick layer of men."

❖ ❖ ❖ ❖ ❖

The great satirist and cynic H. L. Mencken had this wonderful observation: "A man may be a fool and not know it, but not if he's married."

❖ ❖ ❖ ❖ ❖

The unforgettable Zsa Zsa Gabor once said, "I've been married to a Communist and a Fascist and neither would take out the garbage."

❖ ❖ ❖ ❖ ❖

The incomparable Henny Youngman offered this thought. "You know what it means when you come home at night, walk in the door and are greeted with a big kiss and a martini? It means you're in the wrong house!"

❖   ❖   ❖   ❖   ❖

A personal story which I have never forgotten. Marilyn and I were in London for a long weekend. I got a call the first night we were there from the LPGA saying that I was being seriously considered for the Commissioner's position, and that the search committee and the LPGA Board wanted to interview me. A meeting would be held in New York in a few days and wondered if I could stop in New York on my way back to Cincinnati to meet with the committee and the board. That's exactly what we did.

Marilyn and I checked into the Waldorf in New York City where I met with the search committee around five in the afternoon. I must confess that I was a little smug about the interview, thinking that there would be a lot of fluffy questions and that it wouldn't take very long. Was I ever surprised! The committee was made up of players and a few board members and, in retrospect, not surprisingly the group was almost totally female. They grilled me intensely, wanting to understand why a sixty-year-old man thought he could lead a woman's organization. Mary Jo Jacobi asked this question (which, I believe, was the smartest and most penetrating question that could have been asked): "Mr. Mechem, how long were you the CEO of Taft Broadcasting Company?" I replied that I had held that job for more than twenty-two years. She then asked, "How many secretaries did you have during that time?" I couldn't help but smile, and I said that I was happy to respond that the answer was one. Everybody laughed and that was the end of the interview.

Optimism & Pessimism

If everything seems to be going well, you have obviously overlooked something.

❖ ❖ ❖ ❖ ❖

I've been roped and throwed by Jesus in the Holy Ghost corral. (A wonderful country music title.)

❖ ❖ ❖ ❖ ❖

My friends, predictably, always love to tell this story using my name. You can change the name to fit your situation!

A young man named Charlie seemed to have an almost perfect life. He was a farmer with a large and prosperous cattle farm in Illinois. One night as he was driving home from town, he saw — to his horror — a mammoth tornado hit his farm and destroy it. Of course, he was devastated. He decided to start a new life and move to Argentina where, after several years of hard work, he had established another successful cattle farm and he had started a new life in virtually every way. Then, tragedy unbelievably struck again and one day when he was traveling his entire ranch was destroyed in an earthquake. Completely distraught and disbelieving he fell to the ground and pounded his fists and said, "God, I simply don't understand why you have visited such tragedy on me — not once but twice." After a brief time the skies opened and a booming voice said, "I don't know. There's just something about you, Charlie. For some reason, you just piss me off!!" Though it may not be stated in the scriptures, maybe that's what happened to Job.

❖   ❖   ❖   ❖   ❖

Here's a good tip: If you must borrow money, borrow from pessimists -they don't expect it back (this is another Stephen Wright gem.)

❖   ❖   ❖   ❖   ❖

Winston Churchill quote: "A pessimist sees the difficulty in every opportunity; an optimist sees the opportunity in every difficulty."

❖   ❖   ❖   ❖   ❖

My wife and I used to go to a great golf event held in Dayton, Ohio, called "The Bogie Busters." It was a mix of golf fanatics and celebrities from the entertainment world. Attending every year was the comedy team of Skiles and Henderson, two of the funniest people I have ever known. One day we played golf with them and it was a string of funny lines the whole round. Perhaps the most memorable came when Skiles found his ball about 50 yards behind a tree and he needed to figure out how to navigate this obstruction inasmuch as it was directly in his line to the green. As he was considering how to play the shot, Henderson said "Quit trying to figure it out. Just hit it right through the branches. Remember, a tree is 75% air." To which Skiles responded, "Yeah — so is a screen door!"

❖   ❖   ❖   ❖   ❖

Here are a couple of one-liners that illustrate pessimism at its best (worst!):

- If you use a smile as your umbrella, you might get a mouthful of rain.
- Just think   one seventh of the rest of your life will be Mondays.

Passion

It is critically important for success to make every goal a stretch goal. If you get there, fabulous. If you don't get there, you're still going to get a lot farther than you would have had you not set that lofty goal in the first place. The great showman P. T. Barnum put it this way: "If I shoot at the sun, I may hit a star."

❖   ❖   ❖   ❖   ❖

The great playwright Neil Simon gave a marvelous speech (I'm not sure Neil Simon ever gave anything but a great speech) at a Williams College commencement. It's right to the point of giving it your best shot:

> "Whatever path you follow from the moment you take off those long black gowns, do it as though Gershwin had written music to underscore your every move. Romantic and idealistic? Yes. But I can't think of anything worthwhile in life that was achieved without a great deal of desire to achieve it. Don't listen to those who say it's not done that way. Maybe it's not. But maybe you will. Don't listen to those who say you're taking too big a chance. If he didn't take a big chance, Michelangelo would have painted the Sistine floor, and it would certainly have been rubbed out by today."

❖   ❖   ❖   ❖   ❖

This is a good story to illustrate that it is often best to, as Teddy Roosevelt said, "Speak softly and carry a big stick."

The great football coach, Paul Brown, had a deceptively quiet voice for such a strong personality. Moreover, sometimes he didn't speak at all. I once asked Otto Graham, The Browns' Hall of Fame quarterback, how Paul acted when Otto came off the field after an unsuccessful effort. "Did he yell at you?" I asked. Otto smiled and said, "Oh no, that wasn't Paul. He would simply glare at you and then turn and walk away as though he didn't even want to look at you, much less yell at you. That was far worse than yelling!"

❖　　❖　　❖　　❖　　❖

This is a wonderful story to highlight how great people are always seeking to be even greater.

For ten years after I retired from the LPGA I worked with Arnold Palmer, sharing an office with him at The Bay Hill Club and being involved in many of his activities. Arnie and Annika Sorenstam were doing a television commercial for Callaway at the Tradition Club in La Quinta, California, and I was with them much of that day. This was after Annika made her announcement that she intended to play in The Colonial, a men's PGA Tour event. Arnie and I had talked about Annika's decision, and he was uncertain whether it was a good decision or not. During the course of shooting the TV commercial, Arnie went up to Annika, looked her straight in the eye, and simply said, "Why?" She looked at him a bit confused and said, "What do you mean?" And he once again said, "Why?" She realized that he was talking about her decision to play Colonial. She tried to explain as best she could that she only wanted to test her abilities against the greatest players in the world, but Arnie remained skeptical. Annika was naturally troubled by his uncertainty and asked me about it. I said, "I have an idea of how to approach him on this. I'll try it and let you know." A day or so later I was talking to Arnie about Annika's plans to play Colonial. He was still having trouble understanding why she wanted to do it. I said I understood his feeling, but wanted him to think about it in a different way. I said, "Arnie, if when you were playing the PGA Tour, there had been another tour where players even better than those on the PGA Tour were playing, wouldn't you have wanted to take a crack at that group?" Arnie replied, "Absolutely!" This, to me, was exactly what Annika was doing, and nothing more. Arnie understood instantly, and he subsequently wrote her a warm letter supporting her and wishing here all the best at The Colonial. In that letter, he said, "It is certainly your privilege to do what you think is best for you and the game. Just ignore all the comments you are hearing. Do your thing, have fun, and get it done." I guess the moral of this story is — the best always want to get better.

Patience & Forbearance

Forgive your enemies — it messes up their heads.

❖   ❖   ❖   ❖   ❖

A man had a good friend who owned a cabin deep in the woods. Occasionally his friend would allow him to stay in the cabin for a week or two to enjoy some rest and solitude. Late one night, the man heard a noise at the door. He opened the door but saw no one until he looked down on the door mat and noticed a snail. He reached down, picked up the snail and threw it back into the yard.

Several years later he went back to the cabin for another visit. Once again, he heard a noise at the door. He went to the door opened it and looked down and saw the same snail. The snail looked up at him and said, "What was that all about?"

Now that is patience!

Pomposity

"He never opens his mouth without subtracting from the sum of human knowledge." — *Thomas Brackett Reed*

❖　❖　❖　❖　❖

"He is not only dull himself; he is the cause of dullness in others." – *Samuel Johnson*

❖　❖　❖　❖　❖

Augustus Caesar reportedly said, "He wrote as though he wanted to be wondered at rather than understood."

Ponderisms

A good friend of mine — Stan Thomas — has introduced me to a wonderful new experience. It is called "Ponderisms." I had never heard of this before but it could be a wonderful source of funny sayings and anecdotes. You can "google" the word ponderisms and learn more.

I used to eat a lot of natural foods until I learned that most people die of natural causes.

❖   ❖   ❖   ❖   ❖

How is it that we put a man on the moon before we figured out it would be a good idea to put wheels on luggage.

❖   ❖   ❖   ❖   ❖

If a deaf person has to go to court, is it still called a hearing?

❖   ❖   ❖   ❖   ❖

Worth "pondering."

Punctuality

Being on time is almost an obsession with me. Indeed, it led to several "private" jokes at my expense when I was Chairman of Taft Broadcasting Company. My favorite, which I learned years later, was: "If you're on time for a meeting with Charlie, you're already late!"

Being late suggests one of several things — none good. For example. It may mean that you are simply too disorganized to keep a schedule. Or, it might suggest that you don't consider the meeting important enough to be there at the beginning. It might even suggest that you don't have enough respect for the participants to do them the courtesy of being on time.

One of the truly great people that I have ever been privileged to know was Sister Jean Patrice Harrington, the distinguished and much loved President of Mount St. Joseph College in Cincinnati. My friend Bob Wehling recounts a wonderful story about her. Bob was a member of a United Way committee chaired by Sister Jean. She apparently called a meeting for 8 a.m. and Bob walked in precisely at 8 o'clock. No one else but Sister Jean was in the room when he walked in but, nevertheless, she was calling the meeting to order!

❖   ❖   ❖   ❖   ❖

This delightful story reminds me of a not-so-delightful experience that I was involved in as a very young lawyer. I represented one side of a very bitter dispute between two shareholders in a closely held company. The dispute had reached a very unpleasant point and it was agreed that we would hold a shareholders meeting at 9 a.m. at a neutral location to try to end the dispute. My client and I arrived at about five minutes before 9 o'clock, but when we walked in, the lawyer for the other shareholder said that he and his client had already called the meeting to order, passed several resolutions resolving the dispute in his client's favor and adjourned the meeting. Needless to say, I objected strongly. The matter eventually went to court and justice prevailed — That is, my client won!

Rank Has
Its Privileges

Whether we like it or not there is a "pecking order" in life. You don't have to like it but you need to learn to deal with it. The next couple of stories are helpful in making this point.

One of my favorite memories from my time in the Army involves the deputy commander of the Company to which I was assigned, a first lieutenant recently graduated from Princeton. I was an oddity as an enlisted man because of my educational background, and he had a lot of fun kidding me — in a good-natured way. The incident I remember best happened when we were marching with our rifles (the legendary M-1) on our shoulders then came to a halt. We had done this scores of times, and at the moment we came to a halt the lieutenant always called out the next command (known in the manual of arms as "order arms"), which was bringing your rifle from your shoulder to the ground. This time he decided to have some fun with me, so when we came to a halt he did not automatically give the next command. I anticipated the command and brought my rifle to the ground. None of the other guys moved a muscle. The lieutenant came over to me, looked me straight in the face with a smile, and said, "Mechem, you're thinking again!" The lesson was clear: You never anticipate a command. It was a lesson well learned. And, it is a lesson that every business man or woman should also learn.

❖　❖　❖　❖　❖

Another wonderful lesson in how the world works came also happened during my Army days. We were on the rifle firing range. One of the duties that fell to our group was to go to the area (called the pits") where the targets were placed and be responsible for pulling the targets up and down depending on how the shooter had scored. In other words, if a shooter got a bull's-eye, you ran up a particular flag. If, on the other hand, he missed the target entirely, you ran up what looked like a pair of red underwear that were affectionately called "Maggie's Drawers." This particular day, when I was tending one of the targets, the sergeant in charge of our group came down and said, "Mechem, the commanding general of the post is firing at your target. No matter where his shots go, put up the bull's-eye flag." I did as I was told even though some of the shots merited a Maggie's Drawers. This is when I grasped the full meaning of the phrase "rank has its privileges."

This was one of the funniest things that ever happened to me. It is yet another way to highlight the "pecking order" in life. Of all the funny things that happened during my days at Taft Broadcasting, I don't think that any brings a bigger smile to my face than the story of Country Boy Eddie. Taft's television station in Birmingham, Alabama — WBRC — had an entertainer named Country Boy Eddie, who was on at the crack of dawn every day. He was an incredible entertainer and garnered ratings that were astronomical — often reaching unheard of sixty-plus shares of the audience tuned to television. His popularity was so great that the station pre-empted its networks' morning shows and turned the time over to Eddie. His style was a blend of cowboy and country music and down-home talk and humor.

One year we scheduled a meeting of the Taft Broadcasting Board of Directors at WBRC to give them a first-hand look at Taft's most profitable broadcast property. While we were there, Nick Bolton, the station's general manager, asked if I would do him a favor. He explained that they were having a little party that evening to honor Country Boy on his twenty-fifth anniversary with the station. Nick asked if I would attend and present Eddie with a plaque. I said I would be delighted. So that evening I presented the award to Eddie, telling him it came from the board of directors of the company. He thanked me and seemed very pleased. When I got back to Cincinnati the next day, I had a call from Nick, who could hardly contain his laughter. He said that Eddie had come into his office earlier that day and told Nick how pleased he was to be honored, but he said, "What is the board of directors?" Nick said, "Well, Eddie, these are the people that set the strategy and policy of the company, declare dividends, and make all of the important decisions. Eddie said, "I see, but why were they were at WBRC?" And Nick replied, "Because we are the most profitable station in the Taft chain." Eddie thought a minute, and then said to Nick, "Oh, I get it. The tall hogs just came to the trough." I had never heard the phrase "tall hogs" but I have certainly never forgotten it.

Note: I don't expect you will want to use this whole story in your remarks. But I wanted to include the great punch line. Use as much of the story as you need to make your point.

Retirement

There are hundreds of great stories about retirement. Here are a couple that I have used over and over again with groups of all ages.

After a Christmas break, a teacher asked her pupils how they spent their holidays. One small boy wrote the following:

"We always used to spend Christmas with Grandpa and Grandma. They used to live here in a big brick home. Grandpa got retreaded*, and they moved to Florida. Now they live in a place with a lot of other retreaded people. They all live in little tin boxes. They ride on big three-wheeled tricycles, and they all wear name tags because they don't know who they are. They go to a big building called a wrecked hall, but if it was wrecked, they got it fixed because it is all right now. They play games and do exercises there, but they don't do them very good.

There is a swimming pool there. They go into it and just stand there with their hats on. I guess they don't know how to swim. As you go into their park, there is a doll house with a little man sitting in it. He watches all day, so they can't get out without him seeing them. When they can sneak out, they go to the beach and pick up shells that they think are dollars.

My grandma used to bake cookies and stuff, but I guess she forgot how. Nobody cooks, they just eat out. They eat the

---

*During World War II when tires got old and slick, you took them into the shop where a new tread was applied. This was to save rubber which was in very short supply during the war. This process became known as a "retread."

same thing every night, EARLY BIRDS. Some of these people are so retreaded that they don't know how to cook at all, so my Grandma and Grandpa bring food into the wrecked hall, and they call it "pot luck."

My Grandma says Grandpa worked all his life and earned his retreadment. I wish they would move back up, but I guess the little man in the doll house won't let them out."

❖   ❖   ❖   ❖   ❖

Now that I'm retired, I'm still kicking, but I'm not raising much dust.

❖   ❖   ❖   ❖   ❖

One of the most exciting and profitable parts of Taft Broadcasting Company was its theme park division. We built several parks around the United States and also built one in Toronto which we named Canada's Wonderland. Before building the park, we established a relationship with one of Canada's largest and most prestigious banks. One day we went there for a meeting, which was held in their new headquarters in downtown Toronto. After our meeting, the chairman of the board said he was anxious to show us his board of directors' room. We went into the room and it was indeed spectacular — very tasteful and not ostentatious. There was one thing that was immediately striking — the board table was huge. When I commented on this, the chairman explained that the board was quite large and that a table of that size was necessary. He then went on to say, however, that they had figured out a way to use the room for smaller meetings. He then pushed a button on the back wall, and every third seat moved back on a track into the nearest wall where a panel opened and the seats disappeared inside. The table then, at the touch of another button, contracted into a much smaller table. It was an absolutely amazing thing to see, but I couldn't help but have an irreverent thought. I suggested that this would be a unique way to advise a director that his services were no longer needed. Press the button and have him moved backward into the wall. I doubt that this was ever done, but it sure would have been fun to watch!

Rigidity

I like to use these stories with groups that I suspect are not made up of entirely flexible individuals. Or, to put it in a gentler way, are part of an organization or culture not known for innovation or imagination.

Someone remarked that if Thomas Edison had gone to the Harvard Business School we would all be reading by larger candles! The point is obvious. Sometimes we make life far more complicated than it needs to be and we also frequently become rigid in what we regard as the way to accomplish something. This observation about Edison suggests that flexibility and adaptability are great qualities.

❖   ❖   ❖   ❖   ❖

Henry Ford is reported to have once commented, "If I had asked others what I should do they would have suggested that I make faster buggies."

❖   ❖   ❖   ❖   ❖

There is a great quote in the best seller *The Lovely Bones* by Alice Sebold, where she says, "In my junior high yearbook, I had a quote from a Spanish poet my sister had turned me on to, Juan Ramon Jimenez. It went like this: 'If they give you ruled paper, write the other way'." I love that line. Write across the lines. Don't feel compelled to write within them.

❖   ❖   ❖   ❖   ❖

A home accident survey showed that 90% of accidents on staircases involved either the top or bottom stairs. This information was fed into a computer to analyze how accidents could be reduced. The computer's answer: Remove the top and bottom steps.

Self-Reliance

I use these stories to emphasize that, in the final analysis, only you can determine the course of action that you plan to pursue in a given situation. In other words, while you can seek advice from others, you must make your own decisions.

Another Vermont farmer story. A man was traveling through the "wilds" of Vermont and felt totally lost. Happily, he saw a road sign with two arrows. The one pointing east read "Rutland — 7 miles." Unfortunately, the other sign pointing west had exactly the same thing "Rutland — 7 miles." Now the man was totally confused. Here were two signs pointing in exactly opposite directions yet saying the same thing. Suddenly, he noticed an old farmer working just off the road in his field. The man drove up, stopped, got out and asked the farmer, "Does it matter which road I take to Rutland?" The farmer thought for a moment and then, in that classic Vermont twang replied, "Not to me it don't."

❖   ❖   ❖   ❖   ❖

This story was reportedly one of President Reagan's favorites. A would-be politician was campaigning in the hills of West Virginia. He came to an old house in an isolated area and saw the owner sitting on the porch smoking his corncob pipe. On the top step sat a mean-looking dog who eyed the politician warily. The politician wanted meet the old man and ask for his vote, so, he said, "I'd like to come up the steps and shake your hand. Does your dog bite?" The old gentleman said, "Nope." Reassured, the politician walked up the steps and as he got to the top step, the dog growled, then bit him on the ankle.

The man was horrified and yelled to the old gentleman, "You said your dog didn't bite!" The old man replied, "Ain't my dog."

❖   ❖   ❖   ❖   ❖

A fellow named Sam Johnston was an important part of the Taft Broadcasting Company family for many years. He managed several broadcast properties, then went on to be the senior Taft executive at our Los Angeles operations. Sam probably came up with more great lines than almost anyone I have ever known, but one line was truly classic. Four of us were flying in a small private plane from Buffalo to Toronto. The plane had no radar or pressurization. This would not have been a problem on a nice day, but we ran into a very serious thunderstorm. We were being bounced all over the sky with lightning bolts flashing all around, and we couldn't go any higher (no pressurization) nor find any alternative course (no radar). We just had to plow ahead. We were all scared to death but tried not to show it. One of our colleagues, who was seated in the front row with the pilot, turned to Sam and me, who were seated in the back. He said something like, "We've got to calm down. It's all in the hands of fate. If your number's up, you go — if it's not, you don't." Sam gave him a very skeptical look and said, "That may be true, Gene, but I just don't want to go on *your* number." Terrified as we were, we all broke up laughing — and we made it to Toronto!

❖   ❖   ❖   ❖   ❖

While driving, an elderly fellow receives a call from his wife. "Honey, I know that driving is making you more and more nervous. I'm sorry to ring you on your cell phone, but I know you're on the freeway on your way home from the Moose Lodge. I wanted to warn you to be very careful…I just heard a newscast that there's a wrong-way driver on the 405." And his reply: "There's not just one…there's *hundreds* of them…"

Sense of Humor

I have always been a great believer in the importance of having a sense of humor. I don't mean a silly sense of humor, but instead being willing to laugh at the human condition and, most especially, at one's self. As I have mentioned, humor can be invaluable in relaxing a tense moment. Here are some examples.

Many years ago, I ran across a limerick which you can use in a variety of situations. It goes like this:

> He was a very cautious lad.
> Who never romped nor played.
> He never smoked, he never drank,
> Nor even kissed a maid,
> And when he upped and passed away,
> Insurance was denied,
> For since he hadn't ever lived,
> They claimed he never died.

❖　❖　❖　❖　❖

On the first orbital voyage around Earth, John Glenn noted the thought that kept going through his mind was that every part of the rocket was supplied by the lowest bidder. Now, that's a sense of humor.

❖　❖　❖　❖　❖

About an hour north of Jackson in Yellowstone National Park is the Jackson Lake Lodge. For many years, the Federal Reserve Governors and the leading financial ministers from all over the world gather annually at Jackson Lake Lodge to enjoy a little peace and quiet, fresh air, and, of course, to plan, strategize, and share their successes and failures. During the time he served as Chairman of the Federal Reserve Board, Alan Greenspan was one of the most prominent attendees at this conference. One year during the conference, I received a phone call from the general manager of the Teton Pines Country Club near Jackson, Wyoming where we were then living. He told me that he was playing golf the following morning with Mr. Greenspan and Jim Wolfensohn, the legendary financier and, at that time, the head of the World Bank. The manager asked me if I would like to be the fourth. Of course, I was thrilled and accepted. The next morning, we gathered on the first tee and prepared to hit our first shots. When Mr. Greenspan stepped to the tee, he explained to us that he rarely played golf, but that he enjoyed it very much and was looking forward to the day. His drive, unfortunately, was a line drive left that struck a limb of a dead tree, causing the limb to fall to the ground. Greenspan turned to us and with a slight smile said, "Well, I guess the Fed has a new 'branch' in Wyoming!" The rest of the golf game was memorable, but nothing quite as memorable as that first shot and the accompanying comment.

❖   ❖   ❖   ❖   ❖

If you are looking for a unique way to introduce humor into your remarks, let me share a tip that you might find helpful in speaking or writing. A friend of mine acquainted me with "paraprodosians." These are not strictly anecdotes but can sometimes make a point as well as any anecdote. A paraprodosian is a sentence with two parts. The first part is a fairly straight-forward comment but the second part is the zinger. Here are a couple examples:

• I asked God for a bike, although I know God doesn't work that way. So I stole a bike and asked for forgiveness.

• Light travels faster than sound. This is why some people appear bright until you hear them speak.

❖　❖　❖　❖　❖

Puns may sometimes make us cringe or groan. But they should not be overlooked when seeking to make a point. My good friend, Doc Giffin, Arnold Palmer's long-time assistant, sent me a wonderful collection of puns several years ago. Here are two examples:

The King of Assyria was running low on cash after years of war. His last great possession was the Star of the Euphrates, the most valuable diamond in the ancient world. Desperate, he went to Croesus, the pawnbroker, to ask for a loan. Croesus said, "I'll give you 100,000 dinars for it." The King protested, "But I paid a million dinars for it! Don't you know who I am? I am the King!" Croesus replied, "When you wish to pawn a Star, makes no difference who you are."

❖　❖　❖　❖　❖

A man rushed in and interrupted a busy doctor's surgery shouting, "Doctor! I think I'm shrinking!" The doctor calmly responded, "My good man, settle down. You'll just have to be a little patient."

Statistics

I am a devoted fan of a comedian named Stephen Wright. I laugh harder at his lines than at any others. Several of his lines on statistics are just plain hilarious. I trust he won't mind if I quote some of them.

- 42.7 % of all statistics are made up on the spot
- 99.9 % of lawyers give the rest a bad name.
- This is my all-time favorite: Do you realize that half your friends are below average?

*　　　　*　　　　*　　　　*

This is a terrific story to use when discussing how different employees approach different jobs. "There was a construction company CEO who had a job to fill and needed to decide between three candidates. He hit upon a question. He called in the head of sales and asked: 'What is two plus two?' The head of sales answered: 'Three' hoping to get the job and add one more through a change order. The CEO called in the head of operations and asked: 'What is two plus two?' The head of operations answered: 'Five,' hoping that he could get the job and make a small profit. The CEO then called in the head of accounting and asked: 'What is two plus two?' The head accountant leaned on the desk and whispered: 'What would you like it to be?' He got the job."

Success & Failure

Harry Neale who was a professional hockey coach once stated about coaching, "Last year we couldn't win at home and we were losing on the road. My failure as a coach was that I couldn't think of any other place to play."

❖   ❖   ❖   ❖   ❖

Casey Stengel once said, "That the secret of success is to keep the guys who hates you away from the ones who are undecided."

❖   ❖   ❖   ❖   ❖

I thought I had a great idea. Unfortunately, there were two categories of people who were opposed to my idea. Men…and women.

❖   ❖   ❖   ❖   ❖

Sparky Anderson was the great manager of the Big Red Machine, one of baseball's all-time finest teams. When asked for the secret of his success, he explained it this way: "There are five guys on my team who are so talented, so motivated, and so focused that nothing I do or say can improve their performance. There are five guys on my team who are so marginal, so lazy and so unfocused that nothing I do or say can improve their performance. My success depends upon my ability to get the other fifteen players on the team to listen to the right five."

Taking Responsibility

One of the best measures of a mature adult is the ability to take responsibility for one's own acts. We see so much, particularly in our nation's political life, of people going to virtually any length to avoid taking responsibility for their actions. It underscores the importance of the strength and maturity needed to take responsibility.

When my granddaughter graduated from high school, the program included a talk from a faculty member who had been chosen by the senior class to share his thoughts for the day. He said that in deciding what to talk about he consulted with his ten-year-old son and six-year-old daughter. He said that his son offered some very helpful advice, but it was the advice from his young daughter that he (and I) found very powerful. Remember, this is a six-year-old who is just starting school and is learning many new things. When her father asked her what she thought he should tell the graduating class, she thought a moment, then said, "Daddy, tell them to be sure to put their name on their paper." What a beautiful way to illustrate a simple but extremely important quality.

❖   ❖   ❖   ❖   ❖

When I became Commissioner of the LPGA in late 1990, the Tour was going through a rough patch. This led to bad press, and in turn, had a serious effect on the morale and outlook of the players. At the first general players' meeting after I became Commissioner, one of the players asked directly, "What do you think is our biggest problem?"

I replied that I was still learning, but I had a pretty good idea that by far the biggest problem was the players had what I called a "massive institutional inferiority complex." I went on to say that was the bad news, but the good news was that we could attack this problem on our own without relying on anyone else or being dependent on any outside circumstances. In other words, I was really doing nothing more than addressing age-old motivational precept: you will never be any good if you don't believe in yourself. I told the players that I wanted them to stop worrying about the PGA Tour, the Senior Tour, and everything other than LPGA strengths. I wanted all of us to walk with our heads up and our confidence and pride on display. I am proud to say that the players embraced this philosophy completely, and I think whatever success I had over my five-year tenure was based largely on the players' attitude and performance. In the final analysis, the players are the tour. No matter how strong and supportive the sponsors are or the media or the fans, the players drive the success or failure of the organization. And that's as it should be.

❖   ❖   ❖   ❖   ❖

The lesson to be learned here is the need to analyze the root cause of any problem you are confronting and if that problem can be "fixed" by taking responsibility for your actions rather than blaming outside causes, then that is exactly what you should do.

Erich Maria Remarque, the great German novelist and author of *All Quiet on the Western Front,* had this wonderful take on the subject of conscience: "It's always the wrong people who have the guilty conscience. Those who are really responsible for suffering in the world couldn't care less."

Timing

It is an old cliché that "timing is everything." Sometimes we can have an impact on timing, sometimes we cannot. One of the best observations I have ever heard on the importance of timing says that "Timing has a lot to do with the outcome of a rain dance."

Uncertainty of Life

Life is uncertain — there is absolutely no doubt. We can never be quite sure what the next minute, hour, day or year might bring.

One of the most wonderful ways I have heard this expressed was by the great Los Angeles Dodgers announcer, Vin Scully. Vin announced Dodgers games for 64 years and, interestingly, he had nothing but a series of one-year contracts. Vin was once reporting on a Dodgers player (Andre Dawson) who had been injured and Vin had asked the Dodgers organization to give him an update on the player's condition. Vin reported it this way: "The Dodgers organization tells me that Andre Dawson has a bruised knee and is listed as day-to-day. After a pause he continued, "But, then, aren't we all?

❖　❖　❖　❖　❖

What sometimes seems absolutely certain often takes a strange twist. Here's one of my favorite stories to illustrate that point. Some years ago, a fellow who "played the ponies" all over the country was in New York at the famous Belmont Race Track. On the first day that he was going to the track, he awoke and looked at his alarm clock, which read 5:55. He got up, went to the window of his room and looked across the street at a lighted temperature sign and it read 55 degrees. He really thought nothing of this coincidence and went down to the lobby to have breakfast. He had some fruit juice and toast and the bill came to $5.55. When he checked out of his hotel the bill was $55.55. By now he was beginning to think that maybe something miraculous was happening and when he went out to the curb and hailed a cab, it

114

turned out to be cab 555. He began to get very excited. When the cab got to Belmont the fare came to $55.55 and by this time the man was almost hysterical. He figured that after all of his years the Lord or — somebody — was giving him the break that he long awaited. He raced to the ticket window and said, "I want to bet $55 on the fifth horse in the fifth race." Well, guess what happened? His horse came in fifth!

❖   ❖   ❖   ❖   ❖

Life can often be terribly unfair as well as uncertain. One of Johnny Carson's great lines went like this: "If life was fair, Elvis would still be alive and all the Elvis impersonators would be dead."

❖   ❖   ❖   ❖   ❖

Another mystery of life was noted by George Roberts. He said, "The first piece of luggage on the carousel never belongs to anyone."

What's Really Important?

A wonderful, thought provoking quiz on the subject of what is really important in life has been attributed to the great cartoonist, Charles Schultz. However, an internet search makes it clear that Schultz did not author this Quiz. Unfortunately, the true author appears to be unknown. Nevertheless, whoever wrote it had amazing insight.

First Quiz:
Name five of the wealthiest people in the world
Name five Heisman trophy winners
Name five winners of the Miss American contest
Name ten people who won a Nobel or Pulitzer prize
Name the last half dozen Academy Award winners — male and female
Name the last ten winners of the World Series

How did you do? Probably not very well. Now, try the next six questions.

Other Quiz:
Name three teachers who aided your journey through school
Name three friends who have helped you through a difficult time
Name five people who have taught you worthwhile things
Name a few people who have made you feel special
Name five people who you enjoy being with
Name several heroes whose lives have inspired you
I suspect you answered every question quite easily.

The Lesson: The people who make a difference in your life are not the ones with the most credentials, the most money or the most awards. They are the ones that CARE!

❖   ❖   ❖   ❖   ❖

A philosophy professor stood before his class with some items in front of him. When the class began, without a word, he picked up a very large empty jar and proceeded to fill it with rocks, each about two inches in diameter. He then asked the class if the jar was full. They all agreed that it was.

The professor then picked up a box of pebbles and poured them into the jar. He shook the jar lightly. The pebbles, of course, rolled into the open areas between the rocks. He then asked the class again if the jar was full. They all agreed it was. The professor picked up a bag of sand and poured it into the jar. The sand filled in between the pebbles. He then asked once more if the jar was full. The students responded with a unanimous yes.

The professor then produced a bottle of red wine from under the table and proceeded to pour the entire contents into the jar effectively filling the empty space between the sand. "Now," said the professor, "I want you to recognize that this jar represents your life. The rocks being the important things — your family, your health, and your children — things that if everything else were lost and only they remained, your life would still be full. "The pebbles are the other things that matter, like your job, your house, your car. The sand is everything else...the small stuff. "If you put the sand into the jar first there would be no room for the pebbles or the rocks. The same goes for your life. If you spend all your time and energy on the small stuff, you will never have room for the things that really matter. Set your priorities. The rest is just sand."

One of the students raised her hand and inquired what the wine represented. The professor smiled, "I'm glad you asked. It just goes to show you that no matter how full your life may seem, there's always room for a good bottle of wine."

❖   ❖   ❖   ❖   ❖

A wonderful man and a good friend of mine named Jack Lupton was a highly successful businessman and a great supporter of amateur golf. Jack built the Honors Course in Chattanooga, Tennessee, one of the truly best courses in the nation. Pete Dye was the architect and knowing the strong-headed nature of each of these men makes me wonder how they were ever able to agree on eighteen holes. But they did and it is truly a superb golf course. The story that I want to tell involves Jack's total control of the Honors Club. He was the classic "benevolent dictator" and ran the Club with an experienced, but strong, hand. In the locker room is a photograph that I will never forget. It had a caption "The Honors' Club Board of Directors" and from a distance you could see the familiar grouping of a number of figures around a board table. As you drew closer, however, you realized that the face of every person around the board table was that of Jack Lupton. The point was clear and it was made in a delightful way.

❖   ❖   ❖   ❖   ❖

There are many wonderful things about The Masters golf tournament. The beauty of the course, its incredible history and traditions, and the reverence shown by players and spectators alike. One of the most unusual features at Augusta National (the site of The Masters) are the green canvas chairs that people can purchase and put in specially roped off areas where only the green canvas chairs are permitted. They are obviously highly sought after and always filled. But there is a wonderful story — almost surely fictional — about one green canvas chair that was unoccupied. A man was standing behind the rope that divided the green chair area from the rest of the viewing area at a particular hole. He noted an elderly lady sitting in one of the chairs with the vacant chair next to her. This was so unusual that he decided to ask the lady why the chair was empty. He said, "Pardon me for interrupting you ma'am but I simply must ask about the empty chair." The lady responded, "Oh, that's my husband's chair but he passed away." The man was embarrassed but went on, "I'm so sorry, but since I've already raised the question, isn't there someone — perhaps a son or daughter or other relative who could use this chair?" The lady quietly responded, "Oh, yes, there are a number of relatives who would love to use the chair, but they're all at the funeral." This may be fictional, but it certainly makes the point!

❖   ❖   ❖   ❖   ❖

A quick aside. One of the best things that happened to me while we were living at the Loxahatchee Club in Jupiter, Florida, was the chance to get to know Joe Namath. Broadway Joe was a member at Loxahatchee and was around the club a lot. I had always been a great fan of his and enjoyed getting to know him. He was very approachable and lots of fun. Joe had two daughters and he doted on them. When I first knew him they were very young girls. After we moved from Loxahatchee, I didn't see Joe for a number of years, but I ran into him at a charity function in Los Angeles. We both got one another up to date on our lives, and then I asked him how the girls were. He said, "Charlie, they are still the joy of my life but they are teenagers now, and I don't always understand them." Then he looked at me and said with complete sincerity, "Charlie, it seems to me that women are just wired differently!" I laughed out loud and said, "Joe, knowing your reputation, I would have thought you had learned that years ago!"

❖   ❖   ❖   ❖   ❖

A further aside: Our discussion turned to football. I asked Joe who he thought were the two or three best quarterbacks in the history of football. His answer was not at all what I expected. I thought he would list names like Unitas, Montana, Graham. Instead, Joe said it is impossible to answer that question because you would have to understand and evaluate the strength of the offensive line that protected the quarterback as well as the skill and number of his receivers. In other words, the quarterback might have a record that either enhanced or did not do justice to his ability simply because of those who surrounded and supported him. This made ranking them by skill levels completely unfair. This, by the way, is a pretty good lesson for life in general, not just for ranking quarterbacks. You are never better than the people that surround you and support you.

❖   ❖   ❖   ❖   ❖

I ran across a wonderful quote that fits perfectly in this section. The sad part is that I have no idea who said it. If I did I would certainly want to give appropriate credit because I think it is a wonderful statement. It goes like this:

"In life, you will realize there is a role for everyone you meet. Some will test you, some will use you, some will love you, and some will teach you. But the ones who are truly important are the ones who bring out the best in you. They are the rare and amazing people who remind you why it's worth it."

What's in A Name?

I use this story to illustrate how there is always more than one solution to a problem — maybe a solution that turns out to be even better than the first one.

The company that I headed for a number of years — Taft Broadcasting Company — owned the Hanna Barbera Cartoon Company. One of Hanna Barbera's greatest shows was "The Flintstones." Incredibly, when the show was first conceived the preferred name was the "Flagstones." A legal review disclosed that the Flagstones name was not available. The studio was devastated that the name they wanted could not be used. They reluctantly settled on "The Flintstones."

❖   ❖   ❖   ❖   ❖

You can have fun with these made-up company names that might result from mergers. These are not original with me and I don't know the author. I have used these in a variety of situations.

- Hale Business Systems, Mary Kay Cosmetics, Fuller Brush and W. R. Grace merge to become — Hale Mary Fuller Grace
- John Deere and Abitibi-Price merged to become — Dear Abby
- Zippo Manufacturing, Audi Motors, Dafco and Dakota Mining merge to become — Zip Au Dee Do Da
- Polygram Records, Warner Brothers and Keebler Crackers merge to become — Polly Want a Cracker
- Federal Express and UPS merge to become — Fed Up

Worrying/Agonizing

Most of the stuff people worry about ain't gonna happen anyway.

❖   ❖   ❖   ❖   ❖

A wonderful way of dealing with worry is summed up in the lyrics of the great World War I marching song written in 1915 by George Henry Powell. It goes like this:

> *Pack up your troubles in your old kit-bag,*
> *And smile, smile, smile.*
> *While you've a Lucifer (match) to light your fag (cigarette),*
> *Smile, boys, that's the style.*
> *What's the use of worrying?*
> *It never was worthwhile, so*
> *Pack up your troubles in your old kit-bag,*
> *And smile, smile, smile.*

That's All Folks!

I very much hope you have enjoyed reading this book. I believe that it will help you to better communicate your thoughts and ideas to others. So, tuck this little book in your briefcase or purse or suitcase — or wherever people "tuck" things in this electronic age - and refer to it whenever you think it might help. I truly believe it will help you and it will make an old man (me) very happy.

As I close this book, I am reminded of the Seven Stages of a Career which I outline in the Age section on page 26. My career, like this book is approaching an end but I cling tenaciously to the Sixth Stage! And, finally, it seems only fitting to end this book with an anecdote. I once went to the hospital to visit a friend and I thought it would be nice if I brought him some small gift to help to cheer him up. So, I went into the hospital gift shop to try to find something appropriate. I spied a collection of balloons and I thought that might be a fun gift. So, I began looking at the inscriptions on the balloons hoping to find just the right one. What I saw on one of the balloons was truly unforgettable. It said simply "Good Bye." I looked again and sure enough that's exactly what it said. How it got into the hospital gift shop along with other balloons with much more appropriate inscriptions is beyond me. Suffice to say I did not buy it but bought one with the more traditional "Get Well Soon" on it.

So, I won't say "goodbye" here either because it seems as inappropriate here as it did in the hospital gift stop. Rather, let's just say, "So Long — keep smiling!"

Bye!